Becky Jane

Memoir of an Incredible Life

by Nick Delmedico

2017 Human Relations Indie Book Awards Winner

Gold Winner (tied): Life Journey Category
Honorable Mention: Memoir Category

A division of d+2

This book is the authorized biography of Rebecca Jane Bland Eklond Delmedico. Her friends and loved ones contributed immensely to the content.

Manufactured in the United States of America

Becky Jane, Memoir of an Incredible Life
Published August 2017
Revised January, November 2018

ISBN 987-1-58884-015-8

Also by Nick Delmedico:

Sword of Fire
Aliens vs. Dinosaurs at the Beginning of Time
Free the Giraffes

Exclusively on Kindle:

Could You Please Hold My Baby
Corporate Mercenaries
Corporate Mercenaries, The Depths Within

With all love and respect, this book is dedicated to all of Becky's closest friends and relatives.

For T.J.F

As for Thee and Thy House,
thou hast served the Lord.

"...all the gold in the United States Treasury and all the harp music in Heaven can't equal what happens between a man and a woman with all that growing together."

— John Wayne in McClintock

... everything on the earth has a purpose, every disease an herb to cure it, and every person a mission. This is the Indian theory of existence.

-    Mourning Dove (Salish) 1888-1936

Introduction

April 20, 2017

My wife has terminal cancer. By the time I finish writing this book she will probably be dead. Doctors gave her a four month death sentence yesterday. She is a strong woman, but the disease is stronger. I have struggled beside her, as have many others. In addition to modern medicine, a battle against cancer enlists countless allies, but at this time in history, it is a battle that cannot be won.

People don't come around anymore to talk, as if visiting someone who is dying steals a little life from the living. When they do, everything seems dark, somber, and morbid.

But that's not what this is about. This is about life and a celebration of life. Becky decided early on that she did not want to be a part of a death watch. Something she repeated often: It is the quality of life and not the quantity. No truer words were spoken, and she has lived up to these words time and again.

To that end, my son and I decided to take her on a Final Farewell Tour to visit friends, family, and relatives to say goodbye. I decided to capture stories about her, observations from other people, and anecdotes repeated about this remarkable woman who had beaten cancer twice.

Some Backstory

Yes, Becky beat cancer twice, even surprised the doctors with her stamina and resilience. The first time was back in 1981 when she was diagnosed with Hodgkin's Disease. The prescribed treatment was radiation. It was old school. They marked her up with tiny tattoos that were used to line up the beam. Then they pointed this thing at her heart that looked like the laser that Goldfinger used to try to slice James Bond in half. Couple of zaps every day for thirty days, you're cured. Hopefully. Meanwhile you're exceeding the amount of radiation that any normal human should receive over a lifetime. But you don't have cancer anymore. Again, hopefully.

I drove her to treatments every day. On the way home I would pull off the road so she could open the car door and puke. I tried to keep her weight up by feeding her Krystal burgers and sandwiches but most of it came back up. I watched her stamina falter as she grew weaker and weaker. She would ride her bike to meet friends and try to chow down on a Surfer[1] at Ellen's Kitchen, the local lunch counter in Neptune Beach. Fatigue would set in and she would often get a ride home and leave her bicycle. I'd go back later and get it with the truck.

At the end of treatments the doctors told her she could expect to live to a ripe age of forty or forty five. Pretty good considering she was only twenty seven. The only true guarantee they could give her was that the cancer would return one day. It had something to do with the lethal dose of radiation used in the cure. We mulled this over and talked about it. If she was going to die she wanted to go to Alaska one more time. I did what any supportive friend would do. I quit my job and took her to Alaska. That was the spring of 1982.

I won't go into much about what happened there. It would fill a book in itself. In fact, it did. We kept a little journal, *Tales of the Tortuga*, the name of the truck we lived in and drove. It was a grand adventure, one that changed my life. I married Becky in Kodiak Alaska on November 15, 1982. We honeymooned in Anchorage and announced the event to our parents by long distance telephone.

Jimmy Bland, her Daddy welcomed me warmly to the family. Told me to call him Daddy, especially since my Dad had passed.

---

1   A meal, not a person. See recipes under Becky Can Cook in the Appendix and try one for breakfast.

Becky's mom was just glad we weren't living in sin anymore. After our honeymoon we returned to Kodiak and we got a package from them with homemade treats, a small television, a toaster oven, clothes, all sorts of things. It was near to a haul of wedding gifts as anyone could expect.

Our Alaska adventure lasted two or three years. We were both young and resilient. Becky used to say we were taking our retirement up front, when we could, while we were still able to get around. Now that we are old I see how right she was.

At one point we had enough adventure. It had done its job. We felt so full of life and living that the cancer was all but forgotten, the past a fading perspective. We were newly married and embraced the struggle of life. The next thirty years were filled with all the drama that couples try to survive. More on that later.

Then, in the fall of 2013, Becky was diagnosed with cancer again. Stage 3 Esophageal Cancer to be specific. This time the growth had wrapped itself around her airway, attaching itself to the stomach and crowding out her heart. This was the front lines of her battle. The doctors deployed the usual weapons of mass destruction against cancer: first, chemical attacks that could slow the clusters of growth, then atomic radiation to fry whatever is left.

When the prescribed treatments of chemotherapy and radiation were over, not much was left. It was a slow, painful recovery from there, and just when we thought life was getting good again:

April 19, 2017

"The PET CT scan shows something in your lower abdomen. The cancer has metastasized." Doctor Dabhi's deep brown eyes radiated love and concern. He had been treating Becky for over four years, seeing her through chemotherapy and radiation in 2013 and 14. There was a special connection between this doctor and patient, I think because Becky was a dedicated nurse and he respected that.

Somehow he gave her that extra bit of *something* as a professional courtesy. On the other hand, he probably treated all his patients like that. There's a reason he is the Chief of Medicine at PacMed now.

Her diagnosis in 2013 was terminal esophageal cancer. Chemo and radiation seemed to do as much damage to her as the disease itself. After the treatments her systems began to fail one after the other. The cancer was in her esophagus, near her lungs and her heart. The radiation was aimed at the growth, but like a tightly focused shotgun blast, it damaged a wider area. The surrounding organs, the heart, the lungs, the stomach, were all left weak. One by one we saw problems with each of them. Her scarred heart would race and ebb, blood pressure readings all over the chart. They were treated with pills. Then there were breathing problems, corrected by inhalers. All this going on with a backdrop of constant stomach problems.

Becky called it God's cruel joke. She loves food, was overweight at one time, tipping the scales at close to three hundred pounds. Bariatric surgery in 2002 corrected that problem and knocked off a third of her weight. Now, after the ravages of the cure for cancer, she needed her stomach more than ever, and it wasn't there. Like her first bout with cancer in 1981, she had trouble keeping food down. Over the three years that followed her treatment, she lost another fifty pounds, settling in at around one eighty. Most of what she would eat in the morning came back up. Afternoons and evenings were more like a feast. Even though it only took one or two bites to fill her up, she would patiently wait twenty minutes to an hour and take a few more bites.

After numerous tests and experiments, she got medicine for her heart, inhalers for her lungs, pills for her stomach. Then in February 2017 a new surprise, a different pain in her lower gut. An elevated creatinine level alerted doctors that she was close to kidney failure. I heard the nightmare word *dialysis*, but doctors averted that by putting stents in her urinary tract.

14

There were more tests, really confirming what Becky had suspected all along. She knew what this appointment was about. That's why Doctor Dabhi's words came as no surprise. She had been having intense pains in her gut, difficulty eating, and persistent problems with her bowels. Some of it she wrote off, saying that all old people complain about their bowels.

The cancer had returned, a third time now, metastasized in her lower abdomen. Like some kind of insidious beast, it had traveled within her to find fresh organs to feed on.

Her words echoed in my head. *A battle against cancer cannot be won.* She had seen it time and again as a hospice nurse. Now it was her turn to see it from the other side.

Dabhi's eyes are hard now, diamonds of compassion and hope. "We need to do another test, but this may be treatable."

"What's the prognosis?" I ask.

He looks at Becky. "Without treatment, average life expectancy is four months." He lets that sink in. "With treatment, it goes up to fourteen months."

Becky needs to know, "What would that treatment be? More radiation and chemo?"

"No radiation," says Dabhi. "Chemo for three weeks."

Her answer is quick. "I don't know if I could take that again. Chemo left me so weak, took my brain and my body." She mulls through that for a moment, a thick fog of silence hanging in the room. "Fourteen months, huh?" She looks at me. "Hardly seems worth it. I'd come through chemo weaker than I am now, hurting more, taking drugs for pain. Is that any way to go out? I've always said it was the quality of life and not the quantity."

"You can take some time to think about this," says Doctor Dabhi.

"We're getting ready to go on vacation," she says. "How soon would I need to start chemo?"

"Within the next three weeks," he says. "When are you going on vacation?"

"Our son is in the car waiting," I say. "We're heading out I-90 right after this."

His eyes light with surprise "Where are you going?"

"Back east," I say. I reach over and touch her gently on the arm. "I'm taking her on her farewell tour to see friends and family. Going to do a few bucket list things, see the Badlands, Mt. Rushmore, zipline."

Dabhi's eyes raise. "Zipline?"

Becky laughs. "And parasailing. We're going to the Florida Keys."

"I can see you doing that," says the Doctor.

He writes her a few prescriptions, one for pain and a steroid to give her energy while on vacation. "These steroids are a one shot deal. No refills, but they should give you enough energy to enjoy your vacation. Take them when you need the boost of energy."

"What about the treatment? Do you need a decision right now?" I ask.

"Like I said, you should start it within the next three weeks."

One last thing we ask for is a Do Not Resuscitate order. This is a special piece of paper signed by the patient and the doctor telling medical staff to avoid certain life sustaining procedures. No CPR, artificial ventilation, cardiac compression, endotracheal intubation or defibrilation. Becky does not want life sustaining measures. The DNR order ensures that she will not become a bed bound vegetable dependent on machines to live.

I read Doctor Dabhi's report when we get to the car:

> Visit for treatment options.

> 1) Chemotherapy treatment would consist of weekly infusions with the goal of improving your symptoms and extending your life.
> 2) Hospice with focus on symptoms.

> Limit your trip to 3 weeks, if symptoms not controlled then return sooner.

-vic dabhi

He gave her as clean a bill of health, as good as anyone in her situation could get. He encouraged her, nodded with her when she spoke passionately about the quality of life outweighing the quantity. He finally pronounced her fit enough to zipline, snorkel, parasail, and do whatever she felt up to doing. What else could he say? I think he knew that whatever he told her, she would still go against doctor's orders. The greater question probably puzzled him. Would she go against his orders when she came to a decision about chemotherapy?

April 20

We've been in the car for twenty four hours, Nick driving through the night until I took over somewhere in Eastern Montana. Becky has a hankering to see the Badlands and she wants to show me Mt. Rushmore.[2] By mid day we are past Devil's Tower, beyond Rushmore and deep into the Badlands.

---

2   I won't go into detail, but this National Memorial is well worth seeing. There is enough activity to stay busy for days both in the park and the surrounding area.

BUCKET LIST

Touring the Badlands, after the stop at Mt. Rushmore, is one of the
highlights of our trip east. We park at a few
trailheads and I get out of the car and walk a
bit. Most of them are short hikes that lead to
nice views. We could spend a lot more time
here but following an afternoon of touring
we decide to press on.

Our next destination is Cairo Illinois and a
visit with Becky's first husband Jay. We
have been recounting tales of their years
together.

I knew Jay before Becky. He is one of my oldest and closest
friends. We met in ninth grade English class where I learned about
his quick wit and clever banter. Needless to say, we got along well.
Later we were in Debate Club. He was an avid comic book
collector and the first time I was at his house I was impressed with
the sheer volume of his collection. He weaned me off DC and Gold
Key comics and pointed me towards Marvel. Now, that's a friend
for you.

Marriage Number One

Jay and Becky lived in Jacksonville and met in 1971 at a party in the woods while they were still in their senior year of high school. Their very first date was to see Elton John on his first tour. "Your Song" had just come on the radio and nobody seemed to know about him except Jay who had a copy of Tumbleweed Connection. Tickets were either three or five dollars, Becky can't remember, but it was a memorable date. She knew she was seeing someone who would be huge, the same feeling she had when she went to see Billy Joel with her closest friend Kathy.

Jay lived with his parents, Tex and Jane, and their two daughters Ebbie and Patty. Tex was a corporate salesman for DuPont and spent a lot of time on the road. Turns out he had a second family somewhere, but that's another whole story. Needless to say, Jay didn't have much parental supervision, and, like all angry young men of the times, he had somewhat of a temper. I witnessed it myself on a few occasions, but having also been married to Becky, I don't know how much of it was provoked or brought on by passive aggressive behaviors. Either way, it didn't take much to tip Jay's scales.

Perhaps it is kinder to say that Jay is passionate. He is a writer, author of many plays. *Pilate, Comrade Worker, Women of the Dark, The Night the Beatles Played Ed Sullivan, Winds of Change, Just Call Me Andy,* and *Christmas on the Titanic,* to name a few. *Captain Tom* is a musical he collaborated on. He wrote the production for the White Creek Festival in Tennessee, capturing the local history about Jesse James for their annual event. He is a poet, writing song lyrics as well as prose. I personally remember reading two of his short stories that stuck with me over the years: *Old Hankus* and *Donnie the Dildo.* When we were seniors Frank Bull, Jay, and I wrote a musical about the Italian invasion of Ethiopia. Unfortunately, *Benny and the Lion* was never performed despite the number of mimeograph copies in circulation. In 1974 Jay and I wrote and published our first book together called *Neap Tide,* an early collection of our writing.

One thing Becky recounted about her relationship with Jay. It was sweet waking up in the morning and finding a poem on the pillow written just for you.

We all graduated high school in 1971, Becky from Englewood, Jay and I from Fletcher. In the fall we attended classes at what was once know as Florida Junior College. Becky and I had a class together: Social Problems. It was an afternoon class, and after a while she began to skip a few, sneaking off with Jay. Somehow she pulled off a passing grade. We signed up for the next term but Jay and Becky were distracted and crazy in love. They dropped out and were married on March 4, 1972.

Jay was the antithesis of what Becky's parents Jane and Jimmy wanted for a son in law. Jay towers over six feet and adds another four inches to his height with a curly Afro hairstyle. He had his DNA tested once and found that in addition to his Western European heritage of mostly Scandinavian, he is 1.6 percent Neanderthal, a fact he is proud of.

As a wedding present, Tex and Jane made the down payment on a house for them in Atlantic Beach, 309 Belvedere. They worked hard at marriage. Becky was the stable worker, Jay jumped jobs often. Most of his comic book collection was liquidated during this time, sold to pay living expenses to support his growing family. Life was a struggle, so much so that two years after Matthew was born, Becky left Jay and moved to Nashville with their son.

But that was not the end of Jay.

God Damn Tea

This story has been told and re-told as part of the family history. It pretty much sums up why Becky's first marriage to Jay did not endure.

The separation was not a pretty sight. I went to visit Jay and Becky one day and was greeted by Becky and her Daddy loading up a truck with furniture. She moved to Nashville leaving Jay with his record collection, a bed, and an empty house. I moved in with Jay (he was my best friend after all) and Becky went on to a new life in Nashville.

It didn't take long for Jay to miss her, and I don't remember the details, but in the fall of 1975 he rented the house to Joe Cox and I. He packed his things and followed her to Music City.

Time passes on. Becky was hell bent on improving her life and had started nursing school through a tough title VIII program, the kind that we had back in the days when the government supported bootstrap programs to raise people's standard of living. I got one myself in the form of a Basic Economic Opportunity Grant to go to college. Needless to say, the difference we both paid in taxes over our lifetime well compensated the government for their investment.

So, Becky was going to nursing school 6:30 AM to 3:00 PM. She worked form 3:00 to 11:00 following school. They let her out fifteen minutes early so she could start her shift. Matt was a toddler and she was pregnant with Chris. She had to drop Matt off in Day Care even when Jay was not working. One night she came home and was met with Jay's anger.

"Where's my God Damn Tea? There's no tea, Becky. It's simple. You boil the water, you put the teabag in the water and you make the tea." The bitching went on for a while and she made some God Damn Tea just to shut him up. Jay finally went to bed.

Instead of boiling over she stayed awake and steeped, something brewing in the back of her mind. Becky was good at internalizing and redirecting her anger. While Jay slept peacefully she took her revenge. We don't know how many hours it took, but we're sure it was quite satisfying, even therapeutic.

She stuck to her schedule, waking early the next morning and

21

heading off to school and work, a brief stop at the day care to drop off Matt.

Jay awoke to find every glass, every pot, every container in the house filled with tea. Imagine opening cabinets and instead of empty glasses, God Damn Tea. Open the refrigerator, same thing: pots, pans, jars, pitchers, all filled with God Damn Tea. On the stove, pots of Tea on every burner.

We don't know what Jay did next, but knowing the bear of a man that he was, he probably drank the tea and went and played basketball. He did drink a lot after all. Wonder if he ever thanked her for making it.

I asked Becky for a story about her first marriage. All she could say is, "It's over!"

Photograph from Becky's first marriage, found among her effects.

April 22

We visit Jay and get a brief tour of Cairo, Illinois. Cairo is located on a narrow peninsula at the confluence of the Mississippi and

Jay at one of the many historic sites within walking distance of his house in Cairo, Illinois, holding a copy of my latest book *Sword of Fire*.

Ohio Rivers. It is the southernmost city in the State of Illinois. Samuel Clemens wrote about the town in his novel *The Adventures of Huckleberry Finn*. Cairo could have been a major port but racial tension turned it into a poster child for segregation. The main street looks like a disaster. There is one small historic area that the town is trying to preserve and enlarge but other than that it is depressed.

The town has an interesting history, it's worth checking out on the internet. When the Mississippi River was an artery of flowing goods and people, Cairo was in its hey day. That was well over a century ago.

Here's a brief story. On May 3, 2011, Cairo was in the path of the dangerous floodwaters of the Mississippi. To protect the town, the Army Corps of Engineers blew up a levee to relieve stress on the river system. By blowing a hole in the levee in Birds Point, Missouri, agricultural land downstream was flooded and the town of Cairo saved from inundation. I worked for FEMA at the time and it was the first time I'd heard of Cairo. We had historic preservation concerns about sacred Native American burial mounds just outside the city.

After visiting with Jay and his wife Judith for about an hour, we move on towards Nashville. Becky spent a lot of time in Nashville. She has lots of friends and family here. One of them is Aunt Shirley who lives northwest of Nashville.

Becky met Aunt Shirley through Chris, who knew Shirley's daughter. Becky and Shirley hit it off right from the start. Whenever Shirley traveled out west she would live with Becky,[3] and likewise when Becky went to Nashville she would always stay with Shirley.

She tells a story of how Becky would drag her out thrift shopping every week. Monday is tag day and the discounts are better than senior citizen day. I have seen the two of them rock a thrift store. After living with Becky for a few months, Shirley had to return to

---

3   Shirley doesn't just *stay* with someone, she *lives*.

Nashville. She had so much stuff from the thrift store! It was a tight squeeze, but she managed to get it all in the car. As she drove off I wondered what it would look like if she needed to get at the spare tire. Knowing Shirley, with her thrift store treasures lining the side of the road, she would probably put up a garage sale sign and turn a tidy profit.

Shirley and Becky went on the last hike Becky ever took. It was back in 2012, the summer before she was diagnosed with cancer. The two of them hiked with Nick and I to the Ice Caves, a popular spot east of Granite Falls. It's a fairly easy one mile hike. The unique thing about this place is feeling the hot, summer sun warming your skin while an icy cold breeze comes out of the caves. We carried sports chairs out there and Shirley and Becky found the perfect spot, just the right distance from the cave. They sat there all afternoon chillin', if you'll pardon the expression.

Our visit with Shirley is full of memories and laughter. They talk some more. It is a good visit, but it is time to go. Shirley is a vibrant, larger than life woman. Not big, just larger than life. She and Becky hug, probably for the last time, even though I tell her we might come back this way.

"Into the Mystic," says Shirley. It's her catchphrase.

It is a short ride to the east side of Nashville where Matthew lives. Matthew Eklond is Jay and Becky's first son. He was born on July 26, 1972 in Jacksonville, Florida. He is grown now with children of his own and has been settled in Nashville most of his life.

I ask Matt for a story about his mom. Matt tells me he learned about budgeting and money management from Becky when he was nine years old. Becky took him and his brother Chris to Disney World. Chris was four at the time. Becky told them both that they had a limited amount of money to spend. They could spend it eating out or they could buy groceries from the food store and then spend the extra money on a water park or another theme park.

She was always clever when it came to teaching life lessons. Like the time she broke Chris of lying. All kids go through the phase, but in the third grade Chris took to lying. He was pretty good at it, straight faced and well practiced, like a car salesman at a busy dealership.

We had a trip to Disney World planned out. Chris had a Peter Pan outfit he liked to wear. God, how the tourists liked to snap their picture with him. Anyway, we loaded up the car that Saturday and drove a short distance, circled back around and came home. Chris didn't know what was happening. We parked in the driveway.

"We're not really going to Disney World," said Becky. "We lied." She paused a minute to take in his face. "How's it feel?"

It broke him of lying, at least for a little while.

Becky is tired. We stay with Matthew that night and rest up for some heavy activity in the morning.

April 24

Monday morning in Tennessee. We get Becky up and ready for a big day. Me, too, as we're about to do something I have never done before, but always wanted to.

BUCKET LIST

Becky has been talking about zip lining for years now, worried that it will be a passing trend gone out of style by the time she gets around to it. We take Becky zip lining at Adventure Works located at Fontanel in White's Creek near Nashville. She is accompanied by me, her sons Nick and Matt, and her grandsons Matthew,

Jonathan, and Jared. When the managers hear that it is a bucket list item, they let Becky ride for free. It is grueling and she has to hike uphill to the beginning of the course. Several of our party volunteer to go first. It gives her time to absorb the process and build up her courage. We all feel her tension as steps up to the platform and attaches to the zip line.

Off she goes, a Doppler shout echos through the woods as she travels through the trees. Nick videos it all and Matt catches her on the platform at the bottom. Just like that Becky is hooked on zip lining. Her enthusiasm and excitement give her the energy to keep going. With wide eyed smiles we hike to the start of each run.

Becky tells me zip lining must be like dying. She says she thinks about it that way when she is standing there, having to take a leap of faith and step off the platform. What follows in both cases is a ride through a tunnel, one of trees, one of light, with loved ones waiting at the end. "Will I be able to do that when the time comes?" she asks. "Will it be that easy?"

"I don't know."

The culmination of the day, for me, is a dual zip line experience. The instructor says we can compete and race each other down this final line in the course. Two by two the kids and grand kids have at it. When it is time for me and Becky, we ride down holding hands.

Marriage Number Two

As Uncle Bob says in Urban Cowboy, "without [my wife] and them kids, hell I'd be just another pile of dog shit in the cantaloupe patch drawing flies."

The Alaska Years

We lived all over Alaska from 1982 to 1984. Our first job there was in Homer working in the cannery. I was a salmon grader and Becky worked what was called the slime line. A butcher would use a pneumatic blade operated by a foot pedal to chop the head off a fish. It would then travel down a conveyor belt to the slime line where workers would grab the headless fish. Using a curved blade, these slime queens would remove the guts, make a slice in the blood line, and scrape the inside of the belly clean. From there it went into a machine that washed the inside with a gentle spray of water. Fish fell out the back of that machine and onto a table where trained inspectors (like me) would examine the fish and decide what grade to assign it. Grade A salmon had little or no scale loss on the outside and a firm, clean inside. If there were ribs poking out of the meat or bad belly burn, it would be grade B. Anything lower than that went in a tote where it eventually became canned salmon.

I would place the fish on a rack that went into a giant blast freezer. Eight to ten hours later the frozen rack was wheeled over to the case up area where the fish were packaged. Becky and I sometimes worked case up too. A strong man would take a tray of frozen salmon off the cart and dump it into a glazing tank. Here, the fish would be coated in a ten percent sugar solution to protect it from freezer burn. A conveyor belt took them out of the tank. Sometimes the fish would stick together at this point. It was someone's job to stand there and break them apart by hitting them with a rubber mallet. This was Becky's favorite job on case up. "I love hitting frozen fish with a rubber mallet," she would say.

By far her other favorite job was Hopper Girl. The Hopper Girl had one pneumatic knob to move. A forklift would place a tote of unprocessed fish on a hopper and by delicately using the knob to tilt it, the Hopper Girl would dump fish onto a conveyor belt that fed the production line. We used to tease her and say, "Now don't try to learn it all in one day."

This was all hard work but Becky never complained. Well, there were times she said it was cold. And then we smelled like fish all the time, but other than that she didn't complain much. After work, we would go to our campsite, make dinner, and enjoy the scenic view of the mountains across Kachemak Bay.

Work at Icicle Seafoods over the winter was sketchy at best. We took the ferry to Kodiak at the end of the season because we heard there were jobs processing crab there in the winter. We camped in Fort Abercrombie State Park until the season started. The Beachcomber Bar had free spaghetti night and we foraged for salmon berries to eat. With flour and sugar, Becky made them into fried pies, pancakes, and sourdough jam, a kind of salmon berry reduction cooked over an open fire and consumed with bread. We got jobs pretty quickly once the season started.

Butchering King Crab was quite an experience. I wore a thick, leather belly guard for protection, I would reach into a bin and pick up a crab by the claw arms. Unlike Southern crabs, Alaska crabs are slow and you can easily move faster than them. The crab had a longitudinal line running down the underside, a slight depression from their chin to their butt. I would pick up a crab and position that line over a battleaxe type blade mounted in front of me. One push forward and the crab would split in half. I would drop the separate halves on a conveyor belt. There was a little circular piece of meat close to the bottom near crab's sex organs and the anus. This would go on a conveyor belt to Becky where she would pick it up and fling the shit off it. I don't think she ever put Shit Slinger

29

on her resume.

For this work we got a living wage and a room at the Pan Alaska Seafood bunkhouse all winter. The processing plant was an old ferryboat called the *Skookum Chief*. It had long ago made its last voyage, now forever beached on a rocky shoreline near the harbor. Like the *Star of Kodiak*, another grounded old boat, it was converted into a seafood processing plant. They never threw anything away in Alaska in those days, a testament to early recycling.

The galley was intact, a communal kitchen for use by the bunkhouse residents. It was here that Becky learned to cook Filipino food, lumpias and pancit. She was brave, even sampling the traditional blood pudding. It was not a one way street. Her teachers were fascinated with her southern cooking. She taught them all how to make biscuits from scratch, a skill they appreciated.

Once the season was over Becky got a job working at Kodiak Island Hospital. I did lots of short term, off season work: preparing buoys, mending nets, working on houses for rich fishermen. I never could land a job on a boat. We got married in the fall that year, November 19, 1982. After a honeymoon in Anchorage we returned to Kodiak and stayed through the end of summer.

Island fever set in and next winter we decided we needed professional jobs. At the time we had a healthy animosity about Anchorage. "Best thing about Anchorage is it's close to Alaska." That attitude made us settle on Fairbanks, the second largest city. We easily scored professional jobs. I was a substitute teacher and Becky worked for the Fairbanks Regional Hospital. Over the course of the winter we had to move three times.

First we lived in a trailer. Keeping a trailer warm in Fairbanks is like trying to use a candle to defrost a deep freezer while it's running. We spent most of what we earned over the summer on heating oil, and that was just while we lived there from September to November. Then the owner that rented the trailer to us showed up. His job on the North slope did not pan out and he let us out of our lease. We had to move.

Our second place was the Maranatha Health Spa in downtown Fairbanks. We lived there for two months. Becky hurt her back at this time and got disability while she recovered. With a pool and an eucalyptus steam room, it was the perfect place to stay. Warm and toasty, we lived comfortably while the temperature hit twenty to thirty below outside. Fairbanks is in a bowl surrounded by mountains and during an inversion all the smoke and pollutants crystallize into Ice Fog as the temperature drops. We had a studio apartment with a beautiful view of the Ice Fog as it settled over Cushman Street.

The health spa had parking places with electrical outlets, just like most of the parking meters in downtown Fairbanks. Places to plug in your car. I'm not talking electric cars, just so you know, it gets so cold in Fairbanks that cars are outfitted with engine block heaters and battery warmers. Without these essential items, a car wouldn't start. The oil is too viscous at thirty below and the block would crack without lubrication. Also, a battery can't supply enough juice to jump the ignition into firing. Anyone who's started a car on a cold morning knows that it's slow, but at fifty below it's a whole new experience. People commonly blocked off their radiator with a piece of cardboard in winter just to help their car run hotter.

One more odd thing that happens: air in the tires is pressurized, and when a gas is held at a constant pressure, temperature and volume become directly related.[4] Tires heat up from friction as they roll around on rough surfaces, no matter how cold they are. At night when you park, the temperature of the air in the tires drops, and so does the volume. As it settles the tire gets a flat spot. When you drive around the next morning they go flop, flop, flop, until the friction warms them enough to expand the air and round out the flat spot.

---

4   Charles Law, for the nerds that may be reading. The hotter the gas, the more it expands.

As comfortable as it was, we gave up city living. In February we rented a cabin in Goldstream Valley, northwest of Fairbanks. We had to haul water from a well twelve miles away on the Steese Highway. Heat came from a tiny coal stove, and the bathroom was an outhouse that was perched over a fifty five gallon drum that caught the waste. The drum was buried about a foot in the ground, as far as the permafrost would allow. A couple of makeshift steps led to a potty seat with an open door view of the cabin. Rustic but beautiful. We rigged a heater at the end of a long extension cord. When you had to use the bathroom, you would plug in the heater and wait ten minutes. The seat was not an ordinary seat. It was a hole cut in a piece of one inch thick Styrofoam. Did you know that bare skin will stick to a normal, plastic seat at thirty below? But not to Styrofoam!

Our neighbors were Iditarod racers who ran their dogs occasionally. The northern lights never looked brighter or closer. Sometimes we would sit outside in fifty below weather and watch as long as we could stand it. Circles and ribbons and mushrooms of green and blue hues would dance in the sky. You may think that the long, winter nights in Alaska are dark and dreary but nature has a way of compensating. Even the slightest sliver of moonlight would be enough to reflect off the snow and light up the night. Heck, the starlight would reflect off the snow bright enough to see by. All this, accompanied by the *aurora borealis*.

Cold weather is unforgiving. Becky told me about a man they brought into the hospital with a shattered esophagus. He had been out hunting. While warming himself by the fire, he parked his bottle of liquor in the snow. It was well below zero and booze does not freeze like water. When he took a big drink, the alcohol froze and shattered his esophagus. I don't remember if he made it or not.

She also told me about two people who had fallen through the ice and died. Folks liked to ride snowmobiles around in winter, You can't get a drunk driving ticket if you're on a snowmobile, and I used to see them parked outside the bars like a used car sales lot. The bike trails are freeways for the Iron Dogsleds as long as there is snow on the ground, usually October to late April. The Tanana River itself, normally a passage for the Riverboat Dinner and Show Tour, becomes a frozen highway in the winter. Every year there are a few snowmobilers who drive too close to the power plant where a warm water outflow thins the ice.

As I said, cold weather is unforgiving. Experience is a harsh teacher in Alaska.

Spring came, and the snow melted around our pristine cabin in the valley. It looked like a Christmas postcard when we rented it, cute cabin, snow on the roof, a window glowing with warm light. Stars and northern lights painted in the sky with pastel gingerbread, inviting us out of the cold Alaskan night.

Then the snow began to melt.

The trail to the outhouse became a mud path. Worse, the outhouse itself was held up with shims and was teetering over the fifty five gallon drum. Over the winter, the packed, frozen ice provided firm support and a solid foundation in which to do business. Shoring up the outhouse was our first priority of the spring melt.

The snow disappeared quickly over the next day or two leaving behind a debris field of human drama. Standing on the deck I could see a household full of items splayed on the lawn (not really lawn, more of a mud field with patches of Arctic moss). Clothes, cookware, tools, trash, beer cans, a smashed chair, camping gear, even a twenty five pound Butterball turkey.

The former occupants were two men and a woman. The woman was pregnant by one of the men. We know this because we found a letter from her at the bottom of this pile. Apparently the relationship went sour as the two men spent more time together. In the letter she complained about them drinking and going out together, leaving her out of the fun. With a baby on the way, this letter was a plea for her husband to come home and focus on his family.

We cleaned up the mess, read the letter a few times, and tried to imagine how the contents of the cabin came to be on the lawn.

In the summer we packed up the house and moved back to Kodiak where I was a foreman in the cannery. Becky's one comment on the whole experience: "I'm never going back to Fairbanks."

We worked the summer season in Kodiak, living in an abandoned house. I worked for the Moonies, followers of the Reverend Sun Myung Moon. Pan Alaska wasn't processing that much, and as I told my friends, I spell Moonie M-O-N-E-Y.

Moonies had a tough time in Kodiak. It was a rough town, and we saw some things in our day there. I found a dog skin in the dumpster one day. People will eat anything to survive. There were race wars. Fishermen and Filipinos fist fighting to beat all out in the parking lot of the Mecca one morning. I heard about six men being retorted in crab cages. Maybe it was an urban legend, but the thought of people being cooked like canned salmon chilled me to the bone. I heard about crewmen thrown overboard on purpose, so called "fishing accidents," arranged for people who don't get it or go along with the program. All this is heresay, mind you.

Working for the Moonies felt like crossing the picket line. Members of the Unification Church, their official name, were not respected in Kodiak. They came to town, bought a defunct cannery, and turned a profit with it. I heard all kinds of things said about them, but it seemed nobody complained when they sold fish to them and cashed a fat check. I cashed their checks and they never bounced. The Moonies were always buying, even offered a case of beer free with so many pounds of fish sold. They would take refrigerated storage boats out to the fishing grounds and buy it there, allowing the fishermen to turn around and focus on what they do best in the limited time they had.[5] Some said they did that so nobody knew they were selling to Moonies.

---

5   Some commercial fishing seasons in select bays in Alaska were open for as little as six hours.

Working side by side with the Moonies was fun. By and large, like most churchgoers, they were hardworking and spiritually focused. During lunch or break they often meditated or went back to their bunk house and ate while someone read their scripture aloud. My manager's name was Brian and he was paired up and married to his wife in a mass ceremony in Boston by The Reverend Moon. The ceremony was last year, at least last year for 1984, the summer of the year I worked for them. His wife was Korean, chosen by the Reverend, and he would not see her for two more years, a law mandated by the Unification Church. Oddly, three years was also the waiting period for US Immigration.

The workforce was made up of church members with a few local hires like myself thrown in. They had been recruited for the Ocean Church branch. The church put them up in a bunkhouse and paid them very little after all the deductions for living expenses. We, on the other hand, made a good wage. It reminded me of that old song about coal miners who owe their lives to the company store. Seemed to me the Reverend liked to keep most of his money. It didn't work. Also in 1984, he was serving time after being found guilty of conspiracy charges and willfully filing false income tax returns.

Let me tell you about one crazy day I had working there. The City was digging a hole in the middle of the street one day. They hit a main line and the power went out. We had tons of fish to slime, which happens when you buy everything you can. That's okay. Thinking on my feet, I arrange lanterns and emergency lighting.

Shortly after, a knife fight breaks out at the butcher table. The standard lineup at the beginning of the line was the Valladola family on one side of the table and the Sabados on the other side. Both proud of their skills, they would argue all day long about who was the better butcher, but on this occasion somebody slandered the pregnant wife of the opposing family. Honor deserved an answer, and by the time the ambulance arrived you couldn't tell fish blood from human. It was over when I heard about it, which is good because I don't know if I would have stepped in and broken it up.

As the ambulance is leaving, the City, still busy with street repairs, hits the water main. You can slime fish without electricity but not without water to clean it. I shut down the slime line, tell people to clock out and either go home or wait in the break room. I sit in the production office for a moment of peace.

Upstairs is the *sugico* room, a place where salmon roe goes for special handling. This team is entirely Japanese, all churchgoers, their mission to soak the fish eggs in brine and pack them in beautiful, hand made wooden boxes for sale abroad. I hardly ever hear from these guys and only when they want me to move a pallet of salt for them with the forklift. After butcher fights, no electricity, no water, and no production they barge into the production office with another emergency. In near panic, a woman shrieks, "Nick-san! Nick-san! There is no hot water for tea!"

I kept my cool, trying not to laugh hysterically. Instead I walked across the street and got them my Coleman stove.

Across the street, yes. As I was saying, we lived in an old abandoned house across the street from the cannery. The Moonies owned it and they didn't care if we stayed there. There was no water or utilities, not even a working toilet. We went across the street to do our business. It was tough going. We had a window with no glass in it next to our bed. One night I caught Becky climbing through the window.

"Where are you going?" I asked.

"I've had enough of this place," she said. "I'm leaving."

"You're leaving me?" I asked.

"Yep," she said.

She had the car keys in her hand but I took her glasses instead. She couldn't see worth squat to drive and so she had no choice but to settle down and go back to bed.

Things looked different in the morning and she wound up staying, but I always wondered if that's why she was so hot to get contact lenses.

We left Kodiak well into the fall, after the fishing season, making our way stateside again. We traveled slowly, camping along the way. In Washington we rode to the top of the Space Needle, took the ferry across to the Olympic Peninsula, and camped at Deer Park. "Seattle is a good compromise between Alaska and the lower forty eight," she said. "All the conveniences, mountains, nice people, Pacific northwest sense of community. We should consider living here.[6]"

But we didn't. We worked our way south camping in State and National Parks, visiting some of the best sites in the west. We saw Crater Lake, lava caves, active fumaroles, and bathed in hot water springs. It was fun but by the time we hit California we were dead broke. At a rest stop Becky culled the tourist brochures and found some coupons for giveaways at casinos in Nevada, free plays and such. We went through Reno and had ten dollars left in our pockets. What do you do? Why gamble of course.

Becky won enough to buy gas and get us to Los Angeles where my Uncle Joe lived. We cashed a check and had enough to get to Tucson (more on that adventure later) and then back to Jacksonville where we started fresh all over again. It was 1984 and it wasn't long before we had good jobs and a comfortable house, well on our way to middle class life. Chris came to live with us at this time, but Matt went to live with his father in Albany, New York. Things did not work out there and eventually he moved in with Becky's parents in Roanoke, Virginia.

Becky calls Jacksonville her home town, but she calls a lot of places her home town. Roanoke, Homer, Gastonia, Nashville, to

---

6 Twenty five years later, we finally settled in Bothell, a suburb of Seattle.

name a few. Either way, Jacksonville was good for us, it always is. We started with a small, roach infested apartment off Stockton street. After living there a few weeks we found out that our friend Teresa lived a few doors down. Soon we accumulated enough down payment for a house on Hamilton Street on the west side of town. I went to work for a chemical plant and Becky did agency nurse work and life was pretty good. We were on track with everything a young couple needed, good friends, nice cars, steady jobs. I studied for my MBA hoping to advance my career.

Then it happened. A series of bad events that led to a meltdown. We lost the house on Hamilton Street. The owner claimed we didn't make payments for several months and had us evicted. He also claimed the state of the house demanded that he take action to preserve his investment. What really happened was we improved the property, turned the garage out back into an apartment complete with plumbing.

The owner was a greedy man from Georgia who had been given the house by a relative, the man we bought it from. He'd had it some time when he came down and looked at it and decided he could get more than four hundred dollars a month from us for the next thirty years. Teresa's husband at the time was Ken and he helped us get out of the deal and vindicate our tarnished name.

We moved into a cracker box in Atlantic Beach, two semesters away from finishing my MBA. The place was small and Becky hated it. The window air conditioner didn't keep it cold. Our bed barely fit in the bedroom and it was difficult to make. Something stressed our marriage because it broke. In 1989 we divorced.

APRIL 26

We spend more time at Matt's, catching up on the past and resolving issues with it. Becky needs to rest after the grueling cross country trip, or is it the zip lining that drained her? We use a heating pad on her abdomen to help alleviate her pain. Nick has rigged the power plug with a converter so she can also use it while she is in the car.

The family out dining. Left to right: Matt's wife Autumn, her son Matthew, Becky's son Nick, husband Nick, Matt holding baby Victoria, Matt's boy Johnathan, and of course Becky.

After a few days we are ready to move on, but not without a purpose. Matt and Autumn are going to take some time off from work and spend it with us in Florida. Plans are in the works.

APRIL 27

We leave Nashville, headed to Lynchburg to visit April, Becky's niece, with a stop in Roanoke to see her mother. One thing I can say about my family, they love Krystal Burgers. For those of you who do not know what a Krystal burger is: It is a small square patty of meat topped with a dash of minced onions, mustard, and a pickle served on a square steamed bun. Closest thing to it might be a White Castle burger and although they match Krystal in size they are not the same.

The Krystal in Bristol has been a favorite stop of ours for many years. We have often made the drive from Roanoke to Nashville, getting overly excited about the first Krystal on the way west.

The manager understood our excitement
and took this family portrait for us.

On this particular leg of the journey we make it as far as Salem, Virginia. We move along slower than expected and Becky is exhausted. It is almost midnight before we get to bed, too late to greet friends and relatives.

APRIL 28

We get moving as early as possible. Becky takes some time getting up. She is dizzy in the morning. I think, too, she has restless sleeps. I can only imagine what goes through her mind.

Today I hope it's excitement. Our first activity is a drive through downtown Roanoke. For fun, we stop at the market and wander around. I buy a hanging flower basket for her mother, haggling with the salesman over a few dollars in price. Hey, it's Roanoke, settled by Scotch Irish and like most of the people in the South, they know and appreciate the value of a dollar.

Becky wears out quickly. We load up and head for her mother's house where we make her a gift of the flowers. It is peaceful on the porch swing and Nick, Daddy Frank, and I give her time alone with her mother. The two of them sit on the porch swing for hours yakking. It is mid afternoon when we finally go on to April's house, Becky's favorite niece, where we spend the night.

Becky, April and her son Darik, Nick, and Charles.

APRIL 29

"The love...You get to take it with you."
  – Patrick Swayze in Ghost

I realize what has been going on here. As I travel and take Becky to visit all these people, I watch her soak up their love and appreciation of her. Like a giant Tesla coil, she has become a dynamo of love, not only to herself but to all those around her.

We leave April's and drive hard for the Florida Keys. Matt and Becky came up with this plan to rent a place for a week in Key Largo. Nick spent a huge amount of time on the phone trying to book it. I had problems with it going through on my credit card. It's done and we are committed to getting there, traveling by the most direct route to Interstate 95 through North and South Carolina. As we head south on Interstate 73, Becky announces that we need to stop in Colombia to visit one of her friends. She is adamant about it and there is no arguing with her. GPS is great, except that the only route there is on slow, bumpy back roads. The ride has taken a toll on her and she is nauseous from the back road bounce. We have to stop. After all our effort when we get there, her friend is not home. But there is a plus side to every story.

 # BUCKET LIST TIME

This is what I call the Barbecue Bucket List.

We are in the heart of barbecue country and Becky has been wanting real, Southern style barbecue. It seems she has some complaint every time we try Northwest barbecue, and I sometimes agree. They will make great sauce and smoked meat and then serve it on a sourdough roll, or add something weird to the Cole slaw like pineapple or blackberries, or even serve it with asparagus.

Anyway, we hit a place called Maurice's and it passes the test. With fat bellies we head south again.

We critique Maurice's, a local Carolina chain, and that starts a new debate centered around barbecue and who does it best. The yardstick for Becky has always been Sonny's Bar-B-Que, a chain that started in Florida. We come to one near Brunswick, Georgia and Becky pipes up from the back seat, "Anyone have a problem with eating barbecue twice in the same day?"

No problems.

I have a feeling it won't be the last time we eat at a Sonny's.

Afterwards we drive like madmen and get deep into Florida. Nick wants to drive all night but we need the break. Travel is hard on Becky and the back seat of the car is not the most restful place. Somewhere between Titusville and Miami we find a hotel and pull off for a night's rest.

April 30

A slow start this morning but we are off with three hundred miles to get to Key Largo. Miami is a mess. The interstate ends before the city begins and the surface roads are gluts of traffic. We plod slowly through the congestion. We could have avoided this if we had a Florida Fast Pass. The Florida Turnpike does not accept cash otherwise we would have skipped the street tour of the Magic City.

Finally we make it to Key Largo. Matt and Autumn already flew into Fort Lauderdale and they arrive shortly after we do. We are in a two bedroom, two story condo at a place called the Kawama Yacht Club. Our bedroom overlooks a lagoon, visible past a swimming pool surrounded by tropical foliage. The rental includes a golf cart, aquatic toys, and access to some of the best recreation Florida has to offer. Perhaps this is where Becky will do her parasailing.

MAY 1

 # BUCKET LIST

Becky goes snorkeling in the lagoon on the other side of the swimming pool. Matt and Nick check it out first, but then Becky and I suit up for a swim in the clear water. It is a long lagoon with a few rafts spaced between both ends. At the far end is a soft, sandy beach with another swimming pool.

We enter using steps and a ladder and it is easy. The water is clear and we drift among the fishes. It feels like old times. Our lifestyle in Florida when we were young was very water oriented. I wrote for *Florida SCUBA News* and we had lots of easy access to diving. We also dove and snorkeled a lot in St. Thomas. I look at her and she smiles and we share an old, familiar feeling.

Marriage Number Two, continued

When we last left our couple, it was 1988 and they had just gotten a divorce. He stayed in Jacksonville, graduated with his MBA from Jacksonville University and promptly went to work for the Florida National Bank. She went away to the place she always went to heal: Alaska. And now, on with the story:

After Becky left, I lived with Jim Roe, an old friend of mine from high school. Jim didn't take sides in the divorce, he just took me in.

Jim Roe with Becky and me.

November, 1989. I went to my mother's house in Gautier Mississippi for Thanksgiving driving a sports car, a maroon Nissan 200 SX. Sometime after dinner in the middle of the night I left to drive back to Jacksonville. Close to Pensacola I fell asleep, ran off the road and hit a tree. I wasn't wearing my seat belt. I went through the windshield, smashed a hole in it with my head, then settled back in my seat where I woke up.

I tried to start the car. Nothing happened. Then I noticed there was blood coming from my neck. I had a large gash. I knew I needed help. I was in shock, but I thought about my first aid training. Apply direct pressure and elevate the open wound. I pressed my hand against my neck, stood up, and got out of the car. I could see a rest area nearby, bright lights and parked cars. I began to walk towards the light.

I came to a parked truck, knocked on the cab and woke up the driver. He got angry and shouted so I went to the next truck in line. This driver didn't ignore me. In fact, I credit David Caylor, along with Doctor Logan Emlett, with saving my life. David got on the radio and called it in, then laid me down on a picnic table, put a blanket over me, and waited. Pensacola General dispatched an ambulance and a helicopter. Soon I was in the hands of skilled surgeons.

I spent five days in the hospital. My mother sat by my side and was my advocate. The Manager of the local bank stopped by to ask if I needed anything. Friends visited, Jim Roe and Joe Cox. My voice was low and raspy when I spoke. They made fun of me saying I sounded like the warlord in the second Mad Max movie. Girls at the bank were kinder, told me it sounded sexy like Clint Eastwood.

After release I stayed at my mother's house. My car was totaled. While I was in the hospital she took care of all the filings, all the phone calls, all the things that needed to be done. She knew the process well. My sister also survived a horrible accident a few years before. No mother should have to live through it twice, but she did, bless her soul.

Two weeks later I went to Doctor Emlett's office. I had eighty seven staples in my head that needed to be removed. "You're lucky to be alive," he said. "Your respiration stopped several times on the operating table. We had our doubts about you. Your inner and outer jugular vein had been cut and you were partially decapitated. It's a miracle."

Then he smiled, pulled a newspaper out from under his arm and handed it to me. "You're also famous."

It was one of those tabloid newspapers. It unfolded to an article, the headlines saying, "Decapitated Man Walks A Mile Holding Head." There was a ghoulish pencil drawing of a skinny, headless man holding his head in his arms. The article went on with the usual tabloid accuracy.

"They always check the hospitals for weird things like that," he said.

When Becky heard what happened, she left Alaska and came back to Jacksonville to take care of me. She also said she had to leave Alaska, that her presence there was threatening the State. Don't ask me how, but she thought her anger and hurt had something to do with the Exxon Valdez oil spill.

Forced together by tragedy, we reunited, realizing how stupid it was to divorce. I left my mother's care and returned to Jacksonville. Two years later when Nick was born our relationship was cemented forever. We had our ups and downs, challenges, changes in latitude and attitude, but we stuck together after that.

Becky worked on her nursing career and I continued working for the bank. The nineties were a time of bank failures and mergers. Florida National became Atlantic Bank which became First Union which became Wachovia which is now Wells Fargo. I made it through the cuts and worked on the mergers and acquisitions team up until 1995 when another change in life occurred, but more on that later.

MAY 2

We are still in Key Largo enjoying life. Becky has been cooking meals with Nick and Autumn. Nick has been writing down his mother's recipes for his favorite dishes. Some of them are in the appendix of this book, but Becky cooks by instinct and it is hard to translate instructions into exact measurements.

Matt keeps talking about bottling her bacon honey dressing and making a fortune. I agree as we heap portions of it on fresh salad and enjoy the sweetness of each others company. Recipe's in the back. Go ahead and give it a try.

Becky in bed with her babies, Nick and Matt.

BUCKET LIST

Becky drove the golf cart today. It was night and Nick, Matt, and I all sat in the passenger seats, forcing her into the driver's seat. I think she finally gave in as we have been bugging her all week to drive. She hasn't sat behind the wheel of anything in over four years. The last time she drove was when she worked back in 2013.

She was a very careful driver, much safer than Nick.

MAY 3

Becky had a rough night. She had a seizure and she woke me in the middle of the night in tremors with weird, scratchy breathing. I held her and it passed. There is nothing that can be done except see it through. The next morning she has another. And another. I was talking to her and she looked up at me and smiled, then her face paled and her eyes went vacant and she started shaking. Again, all I can do is be with her until it passes.

I'm used to it. She got them when she was young, only difference was she came out of them quickly and with the knowledge that something had happened. In the aftermath she would look at me dazed and ask, "Did I just have a seizure?" or "Was I just gone?"

Those were the good old days by comparison. These recent seizures leave her vapid and mindless for days and she never seems to completely recover. The tremors seem to shake away pieces of her memory as easily as a dog shakes water off its fur. Her most recent seizure was on December 26, 2016. Nick, Becky and I went to visit her son Chris on the Olympic Peninsula for Christmas. Chris and Pancake[7] lived out Highway 101 past the Kalaloch Lodge and down a ten or twelve mile logging road that is not well maintained. It was a terrible trip. The truck we rode in had no heater or wipers and it had a bad distributor that made the engine sputter and occasionally conk out. It rained all the way and it was difficult to see. Nick also lost his wallet in Forks on that trip. He panicked but did the right thing and canceled all his credit cards and reported it lost at the local police station.[8] Finally after all that, there was this dangerous, rough ride over a twisty, slippery logging road, Becky grimacing every bump of the way.

But the worst of it came that night, the day after Christmas. This was Becky's first seizure in a long time, an ugly visit from the past. I awoke to her trembling beside me in the middle of the night. I thought she was cold and I got up and stoked the fire with fresh wood. I went back to bed and held her tight, trying to keep her warm until the fire kicked in.

The next morning I realized what had happened. Her memory was crap and she had this goofy smile. She also didn't recognize me. I could look her in the eye and talk to her but I wasn't sure she

---

7   Her name is actually Terry. Chris gave her the nickname. She worked at
    IHOP and the first time he kissed her, he said she tasted like Pancake.
8   It was found and returned, intact, all the money still in it. There must be
    more than a few honorable vampires in Forks.

understood a thing I said. Empty eyes and a goofy smile.

She took two days to recover. Nick did not know of her past and her struggle with these seizures. I could tell he was afraid. Chris had seen it before and was prepared for the worst. I made an important decision that day.

We had just sold our house and moved into Nick's place on

Chris, Becky, and Nick, on her last Christmas.

Whidbey Island. I knew Becky could not be left alone anymore. Nick worked in Seattle and only came home on weekends. His time and ability to function as a caregiver was greatly reduced. I decided to quit my job in January to take care of her full time. That was over four months ago. I somehow hoped she would be past having seizures, but here they are again, returned like her cancer, a sickness that she cannot shake free.

In the middle of her bucket tour dream vacation.

I lay in bed with her all morning, getting up only to prepare tea for her. She endures multiple seizures. I am afraid. We all are. I call her doctor's office, realize it is more for my own comfort. I kind of knew what they would say. Same as always. The event is over. Nothing can be done. We can take her to a hospital but it would be more for our comfort.

Yes. They're right. Meanwhile Becky shakes like an old house in a Key Largo hurricane. I can see bits of her memory falling away, her past peeled away like so many shingles lost to the wind.

May 4

Becky spends the day recovering, drinking broth and trying to recapture her past. Her memory always goes away for a while after these incidents. Like a dime novel detective I keep digging to find out how much is missing. Don't know how much of it will come back. I can't imagine what it must be like, unnerving, unsettling, maybe even fearful. I can see it in her eyes and all I can do is recount her recent past to her and see if she remembers.

"You have no choice but to live in the present," I tell her. "It's kind of spiritual. Many people strive hard to live in the moment."

"It's not the same," she explains. "The past is the foundation of the present. Without the past there is nothing to stand on."

51

The recent past seems to go first. She doesn't know we are in the Keys, does not recall snorkeling in the lagoon. She can't remember visiting her mother, thinks we are headed to Roanoke after this. I try to exercise her mind and keep her engaged. As we watch *The Young and the Restless* and *The Bold and the Beautiful*[9] I quiz her on the story line and I'm amazed at how much she can recall.

Nothing recent, however. If there is a bright side to this it is that she is not in pain. She has not asked for any oxycodone and she has been fairly lucid despite the gaps in memory.

SIDEBAR

May the fourth be with you. May fourth, that is. It's National Star Wars Day. I wonder how many husbands celebrate this day with the same enthusiasm as their wedding anniversary. At least it's easy to remember.

I like good movies, and the Star Wars series definitely rates. I qualify a movie as good when I can watch it again, maybe a few more times, seeing different things in it, nuances that create depth. I stare into the screen, hoping to and see myself reflected in the teleplay of humanity. We lose track of time and place when we become absorbed in a movie. Books do that for me too.

Back to back episodes are playing all day on the television. I'm watching the part where Yoda trains Luke to be a Jedi, a point where George Lucas reveals the concept of the Force. "Luminous beings are we," says Yoda. "Not this coarse matter."

George got this one right. Sometimes we forget that we are luminous beings. We think this coarse matter is the beginning and end of everything. I tell my son Nick that I don't intend to take anything with me. I'm no Pharaoh, but taking everything you own to the afterlife does not seem to be an option. I believe there are things we *can* take with us. The experiences, the love, the lessons we learn in life, the knowledge that when put to the test, we pass.

---

9   Two excellent soap operas on CBS.

Sometimes I think we are like lab rats and God is testing us. A scientist can predict what a rat will do, which direction he will go in a maze, right or left. He can predict as much as he wants but until he actually does the experiment he doesn't know. We don't even know ourselves. How many times have you said "Oh, yes, in that situation I would definitely do the right thing. If I saw someone being bullied I would... If someone needed help I would..." Predict all you want. I once read a news article about an American soldier in Vietnam who flung himself on top of a live grenade to save a bunch of children. What prompted that decision? Would you do the same?

And so, I think of my wife's decision, of Becky refusing chemotherapy to focus on the quality of life and not the quantity. A very brave decision to say the least. If I have to sum her life up I would say it had a lot to do with death and spirituality. Here she was a nurse, and in the end a hospice nurse. That she should see death from so many sides! Her father died of the same illness, cancer tearing his bowels up until he needed a colostomy. Becky said he stayed alive because he still had things to resolve. Maybe that's why we are on this mission to take her to see as many people as we can before she passes. I have even told Nick that we are nothing but a mobile hospice.

As to her past experiences with death, to see both sides of something. Balance and fulfillment. Can life be more complete? It is her future I worry about. Her quality of life is deteriorating rapidly thanks to these seizures. She can do little more than lie in bed and recover. I wonder if she will recover enough to travel again.

MAY 6

Nick, Matt, Autumn and baby Victoria spend the last few days making the most what is left of vacation. I stay with Becky and focus on her recovery. One day they drive down to Key West and stop somewhere around Marathon to snorkel in crystal clear water. Visibility has always gotten better the further down the Keys you go. Some people might say the oceans are dying but algae blooms, seasonal runoff, and other factors may temporarily cloud the water and reduce visibility. Key Largo is right down the coast from Miami, and it's hard to downplay the impact of a half a million people living that close by.

Anyway, they all go snorkeling off a beach somewhere in the middle keys and report excellent visibility, swarms of fish, and vibrant reefs. Nick says it reminded him of swimming in St. Thomas. I can remember him as a baby, floating with bright colored tropical fish, his fingers reaching out to touch them, only to watch them scatter.

Nick and Matt also rent jet skis. I don't know who pushed the decision but they find a place that advertises the fastest jet skis available. They are brand new and incredibly fast. Nick doesn't have to convince me. I can tell. He walks bow legged and complains of back pain. "Water was a little rough," he says.

We set out from Key Largo after a week of rest and fun with Matt, Autumn, and Victoria. I am tan and relaxed, my body recalling life in Florida. It has the feeling of old home. Becky may not be able to remember as much, but the smile on her face says it all.

 BUCKET LIST

We visit the Coral Castle in Homestead. This item is on Nick's bucket list, not Becky's, but it is noteworthy. The place is a monument to a man's love for a woman. Ed Leedskalnin built the Coral Castle over his lifetime hoping many of his dreams would come true. He suffered from a broken heart on his wedding day. His fiance in Latvia, ten years his younger, rejected him at the alter. She thought he was too old. After moving to America he built this place as a memorial to her, hoping always she would come and live with him, the queen of his castle of love. Sadly, it never happened and now his legacy is a curiosity that leaves people wondering how he managed to mill, move and place all these giant stones using the

limited technology of his time.

Simple. It was a labor of love.

We arrive late that afternoon at Sharon's house on the east coast half way between Edgewater and Oak Hill. It is a happy reunion and after dinner the stories begin to trigger Becky's memory.

May 7

We wake at Sharon's place and the Bridesmaid stories continue.

Sharon and Becky met at Methodist hospital in 1987. Becky worked the Primary Care Unit and Sharon the Intensive Care Unit. They were lunchtime friends that saw each other in the break room enough to exchange phone numbers and information. One day when Sharon went to lunch, Becky was not there. She had quit and gone north to Alaska on one of her many adventures.

One day I got a call from Becky telling me this woman is coming over for a visit, asking me if Sharon was there yet. She told me her husband was mean and to be nice to her and help her out if I could. Sharon shows up, takes the phone from my hand, and they talk.

Some people connect with each other, friends on a whole new level, thrown together seemingly by fate to part and reunite again

55

Becky and her friend Bridesmaid Sharon back in the day.

and again. Sharon and Becky are like that. They keep running into each other. Seven years after this initial meeting we saw Sharon on Northside Jacksonville when we lived on a boat. Later when we moved to the house on Wakefield Avenue, she and her family became regular visitors. Angie and Audra, Sharon's daughters, would come over and swim with Nick in our pool. Likewise, when we would visit Sharon's house, the girls would push him around in a car or get him to play backyard games with them.

We saw Sharon again in Puerto Rico after I started working for FEMA. Again, her children and ours would play. Nick used to complain about how they made him play "School". Funny how they all grew up to be teachers.

Here they are again, the forever bridesmaids, reunited by their determination to see each other, perhaps for the final time. To dip in the pool of friendship, to be refreshed in the depths of what they share with each other, a lifetime of friendship.

Nick and Audra, also in their younger days.

Sharon got the nick name "Bridesmaid" in Jacksonville. She and Becky used to go to a ladies only spa up on Dunn Avenue. One day they were sitting peacefully in the hot tub when it was besieged by a bridal party. The calm was shattered with the chant, "We are the bridesmaids, we are the bridesmaids, we are the bridesmaids." One by one the bridesmaids got in the hot tub with them. There was lots of obnoxious conversation, loud statements of bridesmaid this and bridesmaid that. Finally Becky and Sharon had enough. Their final word? "Too many bridesmaids."

It must have been funny because they started calling each other Bridesmaid. Telephone conversations occurred over the Bride-a-phone. Little Nick even had a toy phone I called the Bride-a-phone because when you rolled it back and forth it yak-yak-yakked. I used to refer to their gossip as bride-a-phoniness.

Becky and Sharon had their own way of talking. It was based on the bridesmaid incident. They called it Jacksonville Lingo – a hybrid of black and southern. When I asked Sharon for details all she could say was, "If you saw Smokey Robinson at the jazz festival you'd know what I was talking about. All the women there

57

knew: fat women, skinny women, black women, white women, Church women. They had no idea they had those feelings and oh my goodness we could have died just then."

I still don't get it.

May 8

We recall one of the worst days in our lives together, the night we spent in a closet hiding from the wrath of a hurricane. It was a life altering day, September 15, 1995. After Hurricane Marilyn hit St. Thomas, Becky was shattered, as broken as any of the trees or houses on the island.[10] Sharon remembers talking to her in the aftermath. There was widespread looting and violence. A gang of men had camped out on a nearby beach and were robbing houses and raping women. Becky said she was walking to the beach one day with a gun and a tampon. She was on the phone with Sharon. "I'm worried," she said. "What if I put the wrong thing in?" Right after that I arranged for her and Nick to go to Puerto Rico where Sharon met them at the airport. She made sure they were safe until things calmed down on St. Thomas.

This prompted a new volume of Bridesmaid stories, their adventures in Puerto Rico. My comment? "Too many bridesmaid stories!"

Sharon gave Nick and I the day off. We went to Universal Islands of Adventure and rode our favorite rides knowing Becky was in the best of care.

May 9

Becky wants to visit the Canaveral National Seashore today, which runs next to the Merritt Island National Wildlife Refuge. She has

10 Read Becky's personal account of the storm in the Appendix.

stayed with Bridesmaid Sharon in this area, and I can remember seeing this beautiful wildlife sanctuary before. We drive down a tour road, Blackpoint Wildlife Drive, but don't see much wildlife. Especially absent are the many alligators I remember seeing the last time I had been here in 2004. Maybe it's because it's mid-day and probably they are deep in the water escaping the heat.

We are going to leave Sharon in the morning. Although she has been very hospitable, we have disrupted her routine. She works from home and has deadlines to meet and she gets easily distracted. I don't blame her as we could spend all day chilling and yakking with her, reminiscing over so many Bridesmaid stories that they would fill a book all their own.

As we were leaving Becky says, "I'm sad. This will be the last Bridesmaid visit ever."

May 10

The visit with Sharon comes to an end. We enjoy the facilities at Hacienda del Rio one last time before saying goodbye. We make it as far as St. Augustine where we spend the night in a hotel. Travel is getting hard on her and Becky is still not feeling good. We go to Sonny's Bar-B-Que for the fourth time on this trip. All she can do is pick at a salad bar. Maybe she is getting tired of Sonny's...

May 11

Becky wakes up early. I take her for a ride in the car in the quiet dawn light. We drive through the historic district of Old St. Augustine as much as possible, then ride over the bridge to Vilano Beach where we try to drive on the beach. It is closed to cars today. There is some kind of operation that the city is doing, bulldozers and front end loaders blocking the access ramp. Later we find out that they are still repairing the beach after Hurricane Matthew struck last year.

Breakfast at the hotel is good. Nick and I try feeding Becky one of everything on the buffet but she eats sparsely. Nothing seems to appeal to her.

On to Jacksonville and another close friend, Teresa. More on Teresa later, but first another item off of the:

 # BUCKET LIST

Blue Boy's Sandwich Shop, Jacksonville Florida. Look it up. Their motto: "One sandwich, one meal," and it's true. They make a two pound hamburger that can feed a family of four. Teresa is with us and we order a Western Bacon Veal and a BLT. If I remember correctly, this was our usual order. The lemonade is great and we sit and swap stories while we wait.

Teresa catches Becky up on gossip and tells us we will get to see Sheree tonight. She is sisters with Debbie who is lifelong friends with another Debi. Becky and I used to hang out with them and the stories start flying. Teresa tells us about a recent visit to the Debbies in North  Carolina where she saw some old pictures of us dressed as showgirls. It was back in 1981 when Becky had cancer the first time. Even though she was undergoing radiation therapy she found the time and energy to make us all Halloween costumes. It brought back memories and Becky said she can't remember a time when we didn't get together and laugh a lot.

The sandwiches arrive and we dig in, managing to eat one and a half between us. Ouch!

Later that night we hook up with Sheree for dinner. Tonight it is

Joseph's on North Main Street near our old neighborhood. We lived on a houseboat on the Trout River at Edward's Marina, now Fisherman's Marina, between 1990 and 1993. Becky was pregnant with Nick and she worried about being able to get off the boat when she went into labor. The tide was extreme at times so I made a step and had it ready just in case.

She went into labor in the middle of the night. I rushed her to University Hospital where she suffered through labor for over three hours. Later she said it was so brief that she didn't get her effleurage or her ice chips. Anyway, Nick came along about five AM and everything was fine after that. Doctors had told us to make arrangements, that there was a ninety percent chance that Nick would be born, live six months on a respirator and die. He was a preemie and Becky's water broke early in her pregnancy. She spent a long stay in the hospital where she had to lie on a reverse incline in an attempt to build up water in her uterus.

Well here it was July 25, 1991 and a neonatal team stood by, ready to whisk him away and put him on a vent. We were all amazed, including the doctors and staff, when he came out whole and normal. He was a little pigeon toed and we corrected that over time but other than that it was a normal birth. I got to hold him first, a rare privilege for the father, and then I passed him to Becky. I can still remember the way she cooed when she held him. It was love at first sight and we welcomed him as an old soul, glad to have him with us as a part of the family.

We called Nick 'Bunner' when he was born. Doctors couldn't tell the sex during the ultrascans because he kept moving and bouncing around. Their best guess was a girl and while in the womb I called her 'Bunnette' since I called Becky 'Bunny'. One day during an examination we got a peek and Becky said, "Looks like Bunnette is a Bunner," and so the name stuck. To this day it is his secret name used only by family, Fremen and other members of his Sietch. Nick stayed in an isolette for a week but then they let us take him home. I had written a poem and posted it on the window of the small baby bed, Nick inside, glowing pale blue under the bilirubin lights.

It was called *Me and Bunner's Mom:*

Me 'n' Bunner's Mom
We go to the hospital every day
And just for extra measure
We hold our hopes and pray
That the little fella we love so dear
Will live to be okay.

Me 'n' Bunner's Mom
Fell in love again, you see
Not so much with each other
(Even though it's true by me)
But since Bunner's here and smiling
Like magic, so are we

Me 'n' Bunner's Mom
Can't wait to take him home
We want to keep him close, nearby
And measure how he's grown
Because we hate to leave him there
In this isolette alone

Some say the world's in trouble
They say that love is gone
But we know better, we *are* love
And if they dropped the bomb
It wouldn't make a difference
To me 'n' Bunner's Mom

He grew up fine. One day Nick figured out how to open the door to
the boat and that was the end of living on the water. I was already
reckless enough. Becky came home from work and caught me

sailing with him in our small Sunfish sailboat. Sheree reminds me that I also installed a baby swing on the edge of the houseboat awning. When you pushed the baby, he swung out over the water and back. Needless to say, living on the water lost its charm when we progressed from a young couple to a young family. In the end we sold the boat and bought a house right down the block on Wakefield Avenue.

I take Nick on a tour of the area before we meet the ladies at Joseph's. The old neighborhood hasn't changed much since the nineties when we left it all behind for St. Thomas.

Joseph's is excellent. They specialize in Italian food but you can tell a good restaurant when the local cops go there to eat. Four Jacksonville police cruisers are in the parking lot. Inside, the restaurant is filled with good smells and warm conversation. Nick and I are the last of our party to arrive.

The pizza here is great. We have a yardstick for barbecue and Italian restaurants are no different. In fact, Becky holds them all to high standards. I have left many a meal and heard her say as we walk out the door, "Well, we're never going back there." Never heard her say that here.

After we order, Sheree starts telling a funny Becky story that jogs my memory. A big group of us went to the Magic Kingdom. We used to get cheap tickets through work for special days at the park. So, Sheree, Becky and I are standing in line for Space Mountain. I don't remember what we were talking about but there was a lady in line behind us who made some kind of connection with Becky. It wasn't a good connection but it amused Sheree and I to hear these two get into it.

When it was time to board the train, Sheree and I jumped in one together and the ride takes off. Becky was behind us with her new friend. "Wait for me," yells Becky.

It was like an invitation to mischief. Sheree and I got out of our car at the end of the ride. I pulled her aside and we hid behind the wall that leads back upstairs for the child swap. We watch as Becky and this lady get out of the car, Becky scanning for us. The woman says, "Your friends left you, didn't they?" Becky flashes with panic and anger.

At that time the exit to space mountain was a long conveyor belt that rode past numerous displays of space themed settings, really just ads for RCA products. One even had the famous RCA dog in a space helmet. Becky didn't see us so she took off running down this conveyor belt, craning her neck and angling her body to see around the people in front of her. The woman was running close behind her, saying mean things as Becky fought her way around passengers staring blankly at the space scenes.

Sheree and I took off after them, close behind, like broken field runners darting through the holes in the crowd these two were making. Every step of the way this woman is following Becky, saying things like, "Don't see them, do you? You won't be able to find them. They're gone. Ditched you, didn't they?"

They hit a wall, a glut in the crowd that refuses to budge. They can't work their way around, but it's close to the exit where the crowd is monitored. Their images are displayed on a string of RCA televisions next to the conveyor belt. It's fun seeing yourself on television. As Becky looks at the screens she sees Sheree and I waving at her. We are just behind her, a small buffer of people between us.

We all had a good laugh about it. And Becky enjoyed how the three of us took off through the crowd and ditched the irritating woman. None of us could figure out why she acted that way, but Becky sometimes brings things out in people that they would otherwise keep hidden.

There are more stories, and left over pizza, but it has been a long day for Becky. We make our way back to Teresa's.

May 12

"I can feel myself getting weaker. I just wanted you to know."

"You're not eating much," I say. "Or drinking." I point to the plastic water bottle on the night stand, my indicator of how much she hydrates during the night. It's pretty full, drained only an inch from the top since going to bed last night.

Couples should exchange better words in the morning, but sometimes I feel like we are not. A couple, that is. The other day when I called her Doctor I was asked, "Are you her caregiver?" and I answered, "No, I'm her husband." But that's not how the world sees us.

Becky and Teresa take a selfie in Seattle.

It is good to visit with Teresa. She recently lost her husband Steven to cancer and talking with her has helped better prepare me for the inevitable. "It will happen suddenly," she says. "I was sitting in the living room. In denial. The hospice nurse came to me and told me to come say goodbye, that he was dying. I was still in denial. I went in the bedroom and held his hand and told him it was okay to leave." I watch her lip tremble as she tells me this. She starts to cry and I hug her and thank her for sharing that.

Nick and I get a break tonight. We are going to see Victor Wooten at the Ponte Vedra Concert Hall. We wanted to take Becky but standing in line would be hard on her and she's afraid she'll have problems which may force us to leave early.

May 13

We leave Florida heading north. Tomorrow is Mother's Day and we are returning to Virginia to celebrate. Becky's niece April is cooking dinner and nobody can cook Southern style as good as April (except Becky, of course). All the mothers will be there, hopefully April's mom Brenda, too, as Becky did not have a chance to see her sister when we visited two weeks ago.

Lynchburg is ten hours away. Fortunately there is a stop in Colombia, South Carolina where Becky's long time friend Cherrie lives. We arrive in time for afternoon brunch and Cherrie has a Southern style spread waiting for us, starting with deviled eggs.

"Becky and I met in rehab," says Cherrie.

After the laughs die down, Becky explains. "I saw her name on the schedule and before I even met her I had decided she was not going to be fun, especially with a name like Cherrie Reeser. I knew she was a big black lady and with a name like that she had issues and we would not get along. I told myself this was going to be the last day of this job, write me off now. Then she showed up, and she was this cute little blond Missy, all well put together and perfect, and I knew that I would never get along with this blonde white bitch who would be a little priss."

66

It's true. Cherrie is one of a kind.

"And then I was locked up in this tiny office with this girl for the next eight hours," says Becky.

"We both worked at Care Unit, a rehab clinic" says Cherrie. "We were LPN's[11] at the time and were locked together for the whole shift in this little office. All we had to do was dispense medicine to the patients."

"We didn't have to assess them or anything," says Becky. "Didn't even have to touch them. We just stayed in that little room the whole time. Patients would come up to the window and we would give them their medicine. Other than that we had all day to yak with each other."

And so, they became friends, the kind that motivate positive change in each other. They both decided to go back to school and become Registered Nurses, a credential they needed to become traveling nurses, the ultimate goal they had their eyes upon. LPN imposed a white ceiling on their careers. Becky tried enrolling in Florida Junior College but got pushed out of the program when she got pregnant with Nick. Unlike her pregnancy with Chris, with Nick she was hospitalized after her water broke and could not attend classes. They dropped her.

After Nick was born and everything leveled out, Becky tried to enroll again and couldn't. Some kind of silly rule about having only one shot at it. Anyway, she was determined to get her nursing degree and researched it fully. There were no internet classes back in those days, so she and Cherrie decided on the Regents program based out of Albany, New York. It was very strict, involving tests and a practical exam at the end. The program had to be completed within a set number of years or you started over. They both signed up and attacked it with vigor.

---

11 LPN used to stand for Low Paid Nurse and not Licensed Practical Nurse.

They would get together and spend weekends cramming for the exams. One of the sites for the exams was Bethune Cookman in Daytona Beach, a place they liked to call their *Alma mater*. The two would check into a cheap hotel and study for two days before taking the tests. They must have done something right because they passed. With an RN, Cherrie was the first to sign up as a traveling nurse. Her first assignment was St. Thomas, an American island in the Caribbean. I came home from my work at the bank all stressed one day when Becky said, "I don't like the person you're becoming. Work is taking a toll on you."

"Coal miners get black lung, bankers get ulcers," I said.

"I got a job offer as a traveling nurse. My first assignment is St. Thomas. Are you coming with me?"

"What will I do there?" I asked.

"Whatever you want," she said. "You won't have to work if you don't want to. Just take care of Little Nick. The company provides living quarters and a stipend in addition to my salary. We could have a good time down there."

It didn't take much convincing. Nick was four years old and I quit my job for the second time to follow her on another adventure. Now, twenty three years later, I hear the details of how this adventure came about. Cherrie had called Becky and told her how wonderful it was working at the Queen Louise Nursing Home in Charlotte Amalia. "It's cute and cozy, perfect for you, more like being with a large family than a nursing home."

Truth was, as I heard the story today, it was quite a culture shock. Cherrie was suffering in Paradise and wanted someone to share her hell. Why not drag her friend into it?

"There was a reason they had to use traveling nurses," says Becky.

"We did all the things that nobody else wanted to do," says

Cherrie. "Like, there was this woman who had a glass eye and nobody would clean it out. My Uncle had one and I wasn't afraid to do it, so I reached in and popped it out. They're not round like you think, they're oval shaped to fit in the socket. Well I cleaned it up, the socket too, and I put it back in and proudly told everyone what I did. They started laughing at me. When I looked, I had put the eye in upside down and one eye was normal while the glass one looked off to the side."

"Spooky things happened there too. How about that old lady who told the aide that her mother had died?" says Becky. "Not more than an hour later she got word that she died."

"I know the woman you're talking about," says Cherrie. "I think she was some kind of witch or medicine lady from down island. One day she was in a wheel chair and she was cold. I put a sheet over her and turned around to do something. When I looked at her again the sheet was wrapped around her head in some kind of turban. She couldn't have done it by herself and it was so intricate. It was a work of art all woven together, something that would take a long time to do."

Becky remembers, "One time she looked at me and said, *They hate you for what you have and what they do not.*"

"She was strange," says Cherrie. "How about the Head Nurse? She went off to that conference, came back and told us, *Did you know that if you have a stroke on the left side of your brain it affects the right side of your body?*"

"How about the way the night shift would come to work in pajamas?"

"Or the times when we would take the patients down to the beach and give them a little rum?"

"Remember that lady telling you that if the baby cries, just put a little rum in his bottle and he'll quiet down and sleep."

69

"And you wonder why most of the island grows up to be drunk."

As I said, culture shock. The tales from St. Thomas, like all of Becky's adventures, would take up another book. Cherrie left the island after six months. Becky stayed. Then we had a day of bad weather. Hurricane Marilyn.

I was sleeping that night when I heard the sound of glass breaking. I opened the bedroom door and saw objects flying everywhere. There was a roll-away bed in the closet and I somehow pulled it out and threw it across the room. I took the mattress off the bed and we spent the night underneath it in the closet while the wind howled. At one point Becky poked her head out from under the mattress and said there was no roof. I looked up and saw clouds swirling, like high speed effects in a Hollywood movie. I used to laugh at those scenes and think how silly they looked, how clouds could never roll around in the sky that fast.

It is human to be proven wrong at times.

At one point I heard the sound of a freight train. It was a tornado passing near the house. I saw the floorboards shake and nails pop up. Becky prayed that we all go at once, that it would be a cruel act of God to take the life of one of us and not the others. Nick slept all night, unaware of all this. It is an effect of the air pressure. The same change in air pressure keeps pregnant women from giving birth during a hurricane. Sure enough, following the storm there were a slew of births at the hospital.

We crawled out from the wreckage the next morning thankful to be alive. It wasn't long before FEMA came to the island and I got a job working on the recovery. Life was good again and Becky survived one more thing that tried to claim her life.

There are many people intertwined with Becky's life. Sharon is one of them and Cherrie is another. Here's one more Cherrie story:

Nick, Becky, and Cherrie on St. Thomas, circa 1996

Nick has always relied on his Aunt Cherrie. She took him for a ride in her sports car when we visited her in Colombia. Nick must have been seven or eight. She asked how he was doing.

"I'm having trouble getting some of those round eggs," he replied.

Don't you know she stopped for groceries and made that boy hard boiled eggs, then chewed out Becky and I for not taking care of his little needs.

Cherrie was dating Rob, who promoted rock concerts. Thanks to his Aunt Cherrie and her connections, Nick had already enjoyed seeing Shaggy, the Backstreet Boys, and now she arranged Jimmy Buffett. What a treat for a fifth grader. There was a special area for the promoters and we got to help ourselves to food and beverage. There were slushie drink machines that you could just walk up to and fill your glass. All this and Jimmy Buffett live.

71

We didn't know the drinks were alcoholic.

Kid had a good time.

May 14

We are at April's house and the stories about Becky continue, like this one: Becky and April smoked a joint on their way to meet Mary Jane and Brenda to help plan April's wedding. They reeked of weed and in the middle of their brain fog they had the idea to stop at the CVS and spray themselves with perfume samples to hide the smell. A store manager observed them laughing and spraying stuff all over each other. They got kicked out but had covered themselves enough to hide the scent. At the meeting Jane and Brenda planned the whole thing while April and Becky got the munchies and ate all the celery and cream cheese.

Becky's refers to April as her favorite human (that she didn't give birth to). April is the black sheep of her family. Becky's sister Brenda married Ken way back when she was nineteen and they had April. They got divorced when she was four and Brenda married Robert two years later. They had two boys together, Brent and James. It didn't take long for April to go from beloved daughter to step child.

I agree with Becky that she is the sweetest thing and does not deserve the treatment she gets. I can see the bond between Becky and April, they are a lot alike. Independent, strong women who take control of their lives and don't let people bully them. Both of them saw their fathers die of cancer. Both of them work hard to improve their own lives and the lives of the people that surround them. April wants to be a nurse like her aunt and is studying hard to make it happen. Most of all, both Becky and April have wonderful children.

One commonality they share is that bit of redneck woman that just won't go away. Don't ever wrong either of them. When April was

72

in high school she used to travel up and down Williamson Road looking for rival girls to beat up. She was banned from Arby's for life. One time a girl in Alaska called me an asshole. Becky picked up a knife and chased her into the parking lot yelling, "Bitch! I'm the only one who can call my old man an asshole."

Here is an April story you'll like. Makes the GD Tea story sound tame, but it also makes you think about the similarities in genetics and how alike some family members can be.

April was married to her first husband Johnathan. Johnathan mistreated April. He had a temper. If she handed him a cigarette lighter that didn't work, he would let her know by throwing it back at her. Johnathan loved his garden, more than April, or so she thought on many occasions. He would go out there and sit with it in the evening for hours, spending more time alone with vegetables than with his family.

April went out to her girlfriend's birthday party at Blueberry Hill one night. She wasn't there long when Johnathan showed up with their young son and tried to drag her home, publicly humiliating her, calling her names and otherwise ruining her good time.

The next day they were working together on their lawn. Johnathan started calling her names again. Before he knew what happened she took a weed wacker and cut down his garden. I mean, everything. Down to the dirt where it was flying, Johnathan came around the corner with the mower and saw what she had done. He chased her. She picked up a rock and threw it at him. He chased her some more but could never catch her.
She'd had enough, got a restraining order against him and threw him out of the house. "He used to come around at night after that. I could see his silhouette standing at the end of the driveway," she says. "He would walk up to the window and peek in. One night I left the window open and waited. He came up to it to look in and I punched him through the screen. He started yelling and I said, *You better go. I'm fixing to call the cops on you. I have a restraining order. You want to go to jail?*"

He left. She finally divorced him. "He called me a while back," she says. "He said he had heart problems. I said, *What the hell does that have to do with me?* He said he thought I should know. I said, *The only phone call I need concerning you is one that tells me you're dead. What the f*? You don't call your son Justin for three years and now you call me with this crap?*"

Good riddance.

The conversation continues, relocated to the back porch. The topic has switched from husbands to mothers. Becky's sister Brenda is a piece of work, or so April says. "One time I moved to an apartment in Lynchburg and Brenda got mad at me for something. She called to tell me she threw away my collection of shot glasses. I had them a long time. They were all packed up in a box, wrapped in newspaper. Do you believe that? She called me just to tell me she threw them away?"

"Mary Jane did the same thing to me," says Becky. "I had seashells that I had collected since I was a kid. I went away on my honeymoon and she threw them out."

"What makes them do that?" asks April.

Becky answers, "Sometimes when we can't think of anything original to do, we just imitate our parents."

April sums it up. "I sometimes think I am blessed to have had only sons and end this mother daughter madness."
Becky only has sons, too. You wonder about these similarities and the influence of breeding over behavior. X and Y chromosomes each carry specific genes with them, kind of an all or nothing deal.

But today is Mother's Day and Charles, April's husband, is cooking dinner for all the mom's. Mary Jane and Frank, Brenda and her boys, Charles' mother Sandy and Becky are all invited. I watch Charles prepare the food. He is a master chef showing me his secrets. He rubs his meat with one or the other of his secret rubs,

74

KC Masterpiece is what he uses on this occasion. I look in his cabinet and see an array of bottles: Old Bay Seasoning, Grill Masters Brown Sugar Bourbon, Badia Southern Blend Seasoning, but not his favorite, Rob's Rub. "That's the good stuff if you can get it," he says.

He rubs the meat, covers it and puts it aside at room temperature on the morning he plans to use it. This is where he says folks go wrong. The flavors have a better chance of soaking into the meat, a different process than if it sat in the refrigerator. Charles then cooks the meat on the grill and puts a glaze on it at the last minute.

The results speak for themselves.

Meanwhile the back porch conversation continues.

"Remember the time Grandma gave everyone money for Christmas," says April

"She gave everyone one hundred dollars to spend any way they wanted," says Becky. "And Chris bought three cartons of cigarettes."

"That was the last time she did something like that," says April.

"Grandma's gifts were always better than Brenda's," I say. "At least they were well thought out."

"Yeah," says Nick. "I got the same lava lamp from Brenda three years in a row. What did she do? Buy a dozen and forget who she gave them to?"

"I remember when Grandma used to give you the same thing as Tate," I say.

"Like we were the same age," says Nick.

"Okay," says April. "Do you remember the year we gave Brenda a salami?"

"And she didn't get the joke."

The Mothers on Mother's Day: Becky, April, and Becky's mother Mary Jane.

May 15

When I wake up this morning Becky is sweating hard. I speak to her and ask her if she wants a hot tea. She never answers, just stares at me with a goofy smile. I get up and fix her tea and when I go back into the bedroom she is asleep.
Later that morning Nick and I go hiking and Becky spends the day with April. They get massages while Nick and I tromp through the woods. Later that night we enjoy the warmth of family. Charles heats up the leftovers from Mother's Day and we feast again. After dinner we sit outside. Fireflies, or lightning bugs as some call them, flutter across the grass and into the night sky.

Before she goes to sleep she tells me, "I haven't seen lightning bugs in a long time. It was dark out there. If you'd have seen my face, it was a smile as big as the night sky."

Pleasant dreams, honey.

May 16

I hug and hold Becky tight. She is getting weaker and I can see it, feel it. I give her tea and broth, the only things that seem to go down and stay down in the morning. I hug her again and my heart is telling me I may have to say goodbye sooner than I want to. This is not up to me, and Teresa's goodbye to Steven rings in my mind.

"Goodbye, old friend," says the heart. "You, who have seen me through countless good times, disasters, sanity and insanity." It is a practice run for the awful truth which lies ahead.

We leave April behind us, bittersweet again, perhaps the last time her and Becky will hug. April wants us to stay longer but we are moving on to Mary Jane and Frank's house.

 # BUCKET LIST

No trip to Virginia would be complete for us without a ride on the Blue Ridge Parkway, and Becky wants to see it one more time. When we lived in Roanoke it seemed like we spent every weekend on the Parkway. Becky's favorite place was Chateau Morrisette located about an hour south of Roanoke. It is a winery with a restaurant that serves first class food in a great environment. Also to see in that area is Mabry's Mill, a great tourist spot and source of old style coarse ground grits. During the summer and fall the place is populated with period dressed people doing everything from blacksmithing and sewing to making apple butter.

In the other direction is Peaks of Otter and the Peaks of Otter Lodge, close to Lynchburg. They have a lunch salad bar there that is good and Becky seems to think she could eat it so we give it a try.

After lunch we ride south to see the Roanoke Star at the top of Mill Mountain. The city built the star for identity, naming Roanoke "The Star City of the South." It has been a tourist attraction ever since. After enjoying the view we come down off the mountain for a stop at one of our all time favorites: Mini Graceland.

As you come down off the Parkway after visiting The Star, make a right on Ivy Street and another on Riverland Road. Then you'll see it in all its splendor on your right. This is not a tourist attraction, but a bantam sized monument to Elvis in somebody's yard. Overlooking the doll sized village is a life sized Elvis in classic pose. There is a little donation box there. I drop in a few bills. Don't want Graceland to fall into disrepair.

We cruise to Vinton and a visit with Becky's Mom.

May 17

We visit with Mary Jane and Daddy Frank, Becky's mom and step dad. We don't use the word *step* and we call Frank "Daddy Frank" because he is every bit the father figure to us as Becky's Dad Jimmy was. Plus Frank loves Mary Jane and takes good care of her. They are both getting old and they are glad to see Becky one more time.

Becky does not remember that we were here just three weeks ago. I show her the picture of her giving Jane a potted flower and she remembers, but a few hours later she forgets again. In one breath she says she wants to stay longer and in another she wants to know when we will leave. Her mother has dementia, and her great grandmother GG had it too. GG stayed with us for a while. She told us a lot of family history. One year we all got together on her birthday at Kings Mountain in North Carolina. The bulk of the family came out of Gastonia and GG's birthday party turned out to be a huge Bland family reunion. My name preceded me and I was continually introduced as "That Yankee Boy who married Becky Jane."

Later that evening Becky's sister Brenda visits. She has connected with one of Becky's best friends from childhood and invited her over and I finally get to meet Becky Beckner. I have heard stories about Becky and Becky Beckner my whole married life. Mary Jane sent us an ancient picture from the Roanoke newspaper of her taking Becky and Becky to see Herman's Hermits at the Victory Stadium when they were young.

Well, as the story goes, when Mary Jane went to work the next day her boss asked if she was okay. She had called in sick the day before and here was this picture in the paper of her taking the girls to the concert.

This family loves to put the feed bag on and it happened again tonight. Becky's sister Brenda and her husband Robert show up, and so do April and Darik in a surprise visit. Full spread, including green beans, salad, squash casserole, boiled potatoes in butter, and corn on the cob.

Nick and I had hiked McAfee's Knob earlier and were hungry and tired. It's a twelve mile round trip well worth the walk, as you can tell by the picture to the right. I can't remember the last time I walked that far. Oh, yeah. Universal Studios Islands of Adventure last month. Funny, it didn't seem as far.

day, February 17, 1984   Reviews ● Comics ● Puzzles ● Columns ● Features ● TV Schedules

I could Not Believe this when it came out last week

The sun and some 5,000 fans turned out when Herman's Hermits made a second visit to Roanoke

The promoters boosted rock

. . . And one took a bath when weather turned bad

By JOE KENNEDY
Staff writer

Pete Apostolou will never forget it. The longtime Roanoke promoter calls it "my biggest fiasco."

It happened May 22, 1965, at Roanoke's Victory Stadium.

It featured Herman's Hermits, then the biggest rock 'n' roll act going, a large crowd and a rainstorm that wouldn't quit.

"It was a plain fiasco."

Apostolou, a short, bald man, even then knew his way to the bank, but he...

Concert was washed out the first time Hermits came to Roanoke

A reprint of the infamous Hermit's Hermits article that got Mary Jane in trouble. She is in the lower picture to the right, one hand on a purse covering her head from the rain, the other gripping Becky tight. Becky Beckner is just behind.

Dinner is a welcome treat. During dinner Brenda announces that she loves to do dishes, but when the dinner is over she disappears into the bedroom where the girls all lay on the bed and yak.

Nick and Mary Jane did the dishes.

May 18

I wake Nick up early this morning and he makes breakfast for everyone. Becky has taught him well and he has gravy down, even Mary Jane had to admit it.

Brenda's son James works for UPS and we want to see him before we leave town. The last time we saw any of our Roanoke nephews was Christmas 2004 before we left for Seattle. We keep up with them. James enlisted, did a tour in the Middle East, and we are all proud of him. Brent went to college, married, and is working.

We want to see James so Brenda has this idea that we can go and meet him somewhere on his delivery route. Great idea if we could keep up with her. She zooms through Vinton, a town I always heard to be careful in. Brenda leads us on a wild goose chase that ends with us taking a wrong turn and following the wrong UPS truck. You have to wonder if it is on purpose as it seems she is always trying to make Becky look like a fool. No wonder they don't get along.

Becky and Brenda looking so happy together.

May 19

Our last day in Virginia.

Proof that Nick knows gravy. When she gets up this morning, Mary Jane asks, "Where's breakfast? Is something wrong with Nicholas?"

Mary Jane and Daddy Frank go with us to market square in downtown Roanoke. Becky has her mind set on a chili dog and if she thinks she can eat it I will buy her one. Problem is, she, Jane, and Frank have mobility problems, so Nick and I walk the few blocks to Texas Tavern to get two chili dogs. They go down easy and everyone is satisfied. As we part I see Mary Jane crying. Parents should not outlive their children and it has been tough enough on her losing Becky's Dad to Cancer twelve years ago.

Our next stop is Katie-Scarlett in Winston-Salem and yes she is named after the famous *Gone With The Wind* character. Debi, her Mom, is riding over from Hayesville, North Carolina where she lives now. Debi, as you recall, is a friend of Teresa's.[12] Katie Scarlett and  Little Nick were born months apart and Becky and Debi pledged that when they grew up their children would be wed.

Well, it didn't happen. Both of them are 25 and Katie-Scarlett is married to Brad and has a three month old baby named Eli. We spend time reminiscing. Debi brought a bunch of pictures, many of them from parties we had when we were young. We recall a Halloween party that was Dune themed. Becky was a Bene-

---

12 Go back to May 11 if you missed Teresa and want some background on Debi.

Gesserit and I wore a stillsuit and our friend Steve Harmon who was staying with us dressed as a Sardukaur Captain. We made a sandworm pinata which everyone said looked like a giant penis. Maybe it was the tone set from the beginning. Lindsay came as Vanna White and we played a game of Wheel of Fortune with suggestive answers. It didn't help that Joe answered the first puzzle just like a contestant saying "It's-all-pink-on-the-in-side." It was one of our parties that got out of control and I prefer to leave it at that. A good time was had by all.

A party to remember as Lindsay, dressed as Vanna White, reveals a very revealing answer to a puzzle. Becky is to the right in her Bene Gesserit costume.

Debi has pictures from another party where Becky went as Oprah Winfrey and I went as Mother Nature. Nick gets a full dose of the insanity of our youth, but we haven't kept too many secrets from him since he's come of age. Debi reminds me that I also did an Astrology chart on her when she was young. I barely remember, but there was a time in my life when I lived with my friend Chris and we studied metaphysics. I was licensed to teach and practice Astrology, Palmistry, and Numerology by the *Cosmic Church of Truth* in Jacksonville, run by Reverend and Mrs. Tunks. Debi's mother, Sue Steinhauser, was a mentor to us and she used to host a weekly class in her home where we would review and discuss philosophy, religion, and life in general.

Debi tells me a number of my predictions came true, especially one I made concerning problems she would have with her feet when she got older. I am shy about the psychic arts anymore and instead I focus effort on my own spiritual growth and development. Lately I like to read Edgar Cayce, an author that Becky's Dad turned me on to.

Nick is looking at a copy of an old Astrology book that I gave Debi called Linda Goodman's Sun Signs. He is amazed at the accuracy of the writing and doesn't know what to think. He takes pictures of the text with his phone so he can read it later when he can digest it.

We swap stories and view more pictures and then head to a barbecue restaurant in downtown Winston. It seems we are again researching barbecue and the debate is on as we try Carolina style smoked meat. Becky talks a lot about RO's in Gastonia. I went there with her once and it was all pork so I asked for a slaw dog and they brought me a hot dog bun filled with cole slaw. When I asked them about the hot dog the lady looked at me like I was crazy and said, "Well if ya' wanted a weenie ya shoulda asked for one."

What do I know about Carolina barbecue? Like I've said before, I'm just that Yankee Boy who married Becky Jane.

May 20

My brother Tony and his wife Hope are mental health counselors, soon to be Psychiatrists when they finish up their dissertations. It comes naturally. As we sit and talk Tony falls easily into his routine.

"Tell us a little about yourself," he says, as if leading a circle.

Did I mention he has a wry sense of humor?

I find that he and I have the same coping mechanisms. Humor is our main defense. He points out that if we laugh at something dreadfully serious, then we don't have to talk about it in that dark tone of voice. "It's like scuba diving," he says. "You go down to the depths, explore, then return to the surface. At a funeral for example, we cry, go down to that dark place, then laugh, cry again, laugh, and so on, up and down, in and out until we have touched the depths within us enough to know what's there. It's healthy. I don't know, are there any other organisms on the planet that laugh?"

The Delmedico Family Band hard at work.

Research shows that some animals exhibit laughter like vocalizations, but is it the same? The closest we come to is whales. They have spindle cells in their brains which are associated with decision making and emotions.

Becky explains her predicament. "You can tell me something and ten minutes later I will forget it."

"Really?" says Tony. "You should have heard what Nick said about you ten minutes ago."

Humor. It runs in the family.

Nick loves to play his tuba but there is no room for one on this trip. Tony decides to surprise him by borrowing a tuba from someone. The result is an impromptu band.

May 21

When I ask Tony for his favorite Becky story he says it had to be the time he was the best man at our third wedding. Yes, Becky and I have been married three times. The first was in Kodiak Alaska on November 19, 1982. Steve Harmon was the best man and if Georgia, his friend, hadn't come with us we wouldn't have had a wedding party. I don't know who would have signed as the second witness. We went before the Justice of the Peace and as we ascended the stairs to the courtroom we met a couple that had just been wed. They both had smiles as big as ours and I guess that was an indicator because the bride asked, "Are you getting married?"

"Yes," I said.

"Congratulations," said the groom.

"Where are your flowers?" asked the bride.

"We don't have any," I said. She smiled and gave Becky her

flowers.

When it came to the part of the ceremony where I was supposed to produce a ring, well that was nonexistent too. The judge was a old pro and must have encountered this awkward moment more than a few times because he didn't even break stride and the ceremony was completed without a hitch. Oops, I meant with a hitch.

We had problems in 1989, but you already know that. I won't go into too many details, needless to say life was miserable and our marriage did not survive that year. I had a friend, Ray, who was a lawyer and he arranged the divorce. It happened so quickly Becky did not have time to react. Ray said later that he viewed it as one of the biggest regrets of his career. Well, as the story goes, she went her way and I went mine. I eventually bought a houseboat and moved away from the Jacksonville Beaches to live on the Trout River. Becky showed up sometime the following year with her son Chris and got an apartment nearby. We started seeing each other and, well, to make this brief, she got pregnant with Nick. [13] Anyway you already heard the rest of this story. When Becky went into the hospital for doctor ordered bed rest, I closed down her apartment and moved Chris and her onto the boat.

Chris was starting to break bad at this time. One day Becky and Bridesmaid Sharon were riding around. Sharon pointed to two teenagers walking down the roadside smoking cigarettes.

"Aren't you glad they're not your kids," she said.

One of them turned out to be Chris. I was not there but as Bridesmaid tells the story, she stopped that car and watched Becky get out and slap the cigarette out of his hand and brow beat him into the car. Turns out he had been skipping school and having a wild time with one of his buddies. It wasn't long after that he stole a bunch of money from Becky and took my truck to Virginia to see grandma. When it was all over the judge sentenced him to six Jacksonville Suns baseball games. Becky put him in a Christian

_____

13 You already read the story of his birth. See May 11 if you forgot.

school and would drive him across town every morning to attend classes. It didn't work and eventually he got caught shoplifting. We managed to get him out of that one but in the end he went to live in Albany, New York with Jay and his new wife Judy. We went on to happier times. Soon we were no longer acting like a divorced couple. Having a baby made us grow up and act like adults.

The second wedding occurred in St. Thomas on November 19, 1995. It was shortly after Hurricane Marilyn. Spending the night huddled under a mattress while the wrath of the storm loosed itself on the world changed our perspective. It was time to forget the past and rededicate our marriage.

Our friend Eric had a different take on it and commented, "I thought people grew closer and got married after spending time together on top of a mattress."

While Nick and Becky were safely away on Puerto Rico, I planned a secret proposal followed by a quick wedding, all in one day. How could she say no? The day had to be November 19. I was not going to force myself to remember two wedding anniversary dates, guys have enough trouble with one.

We held a party on the beach at Hull Bay. Becky thought it was a FEMA party, especially since I had invited a lot of people from work. They all knew what was going to happen. At one point I got down on one knee, produced a ring and popped the question. Becky was in disbelief but I had a minister standing by in the crowd. Still in disbelief, I had the minister come forward and confirm the truth. We had a simple ceremony on the beach, all of us in bathing suits. The bride wore black spandex, the groom blue. I sang Some Enchanted Evening, one of a repertoire that we can pull from a list and claim as Our Song. My friend Harry was the best man and there were no women at the party so Eric acted as a proxy for Cherrie who would have been the Maid of Honor if she hadn't left St. Thomas already.

It was a sweet ceremony. Eric had brought a bottle of Dom and with no glasses we passed it around, everyone taking a poke from the bottle. Afterwards Becky and I went scuba diving. Guests said that shortly after they observed a giant wave hit the beach. They took it as a sign that the marriage had been consummated. I was in bliss, holding my love's hand as we wandered through coral canyons teeming with life. I guess I would have to say that it was my idea of a perfect wedding. How often does the groom get to decide all these things?

Maybe that's why there was a problem with the paperwork from that wedding. Man-planning is often big picture and does not include the fine details, figuring that everything will work out in the end. But this was not a minor detail, and after a while we realized that we were not officially married. Now you see why we needed a third wedding.

The date was etched in stone. It had to be November 19. I don't know how we decided on Vegas, but that was the place: Chapel of the Flowers. Becky made the arrangements, I was deployed to Orlando in response to the four hurricanes that struck Florida in 2003. All I had to do was arrange time off from work.

A week in Vegas. What happens in Vegas stays in Vegas, but that's not always the case. Many were invited but few attended. Nick was in school so he was not there even though he wanted to come. The wedding party was small. As stated before, my brother Tony was the Best Man and Cherrie was the Maid of Honor. Steven and Teresa were there, and Eric, Proxy Maid of Honor from our second wedding in St. Thomas. The ceremony was performed by Elvis. Well, an Elvis impersonator. A little side note: Elvis does not actually marry you, at least not every Elvis impersonator. I don't know if any of them are ordained ministers or licensed in Nevada to perform weddings. We were actually married in the back room by a real minister, then escorted to the chapel where Elvis and the wedding party were waiting.

It was a wonderful ceremony, full of fun and laughter. Elvis was a hoot and kept making passes at Cherrie. He also sang songs, *Love*

Me Tender, I Can't Help Falling in Love With You, and *I Want You, I Need You, I Love You*. At the end of the wedding after Elvis pronounced us man and wife, the groomsmen and I whipped out some plastic Elvis glasses complete with sideburns, put them on and I said (in my best Elvis impersonator voice), "Thank you. Thank you very much."

The ceremony was broadcast live on the internet. We have a copy but it's in storage. When we get back to Seattle I will upload it on YouTube as *Nick and Becky Delmedico's Elvis Wedding*. If you've never seen a Vegas Elvis wedding, it's worth a look.

After the wedding we got a limo ride to the Stratosphere where the reception was held. Tony remembered us going upstairs afterward to ride some crazy thing that dangled you over the side. I remember two Asian ladies asking me to pose for a picture with them. Later as we left the Stratosphere we met a couple (obviously drunk) who stopped us and asked us if we were married.

"Yes," said Becky.

"Was it easy?" she asked.

"Yes," I said. "There are places all over town to get married. You just have to go to City Hall and get a marriage license first."

"Does it cost anything?" he asked.

"Fifty dollars," I said.

He looked at her for a minute and said, "Aw, hell. Let's just go get the buffet."

May 22

This morning we are recalling Daddy's funeral. I had forgotten about Daddy's funeral. In my entire life I have not seen an event like this, nor will I ever again. James Bland got an old time Southern sendoff like I'd never seen.

I knew something big was up when we were at the funeral home chapel when Brother Larry was setting the stage. "We'll put the choir over here," he said, waving his arms. "The organ can set here and we'll put the pie-ano over here."

Brother Larry is a charismatic preacher complete with a booming voice of thunder. I'd been to church with the family and witnessed it first hand. When he lifted his hand up high and made it tremble, the spotlights would reflect off the diamond rings he wore and light the church up like a disco ball. He wore expensive suits and drove a Cadillac. His wife was always dressed in finery. One time during a sermon he thanked the congregation for buying him a hunting rifle. He talked about his hunting trip in Pennsylvania and his successes at deer hunting.

Chris leaned over and whispered to me, "Do all preachers like to kill God's creatures?"

I would have no problem with this except Brother Larry's congregation was poor. It does not seem right in my opinion to flaunt wealth in front of people who have nothing. It is a basic problem I have with organized religion. I was raised devout Catholic. My mother and father separated early in their marriage. My mother was broke and went to the church for help. They denied her and told her to look elsewhere.

"What about the money we put in the poor box every week?" she asked.

"Oh," said the priest. "We use that to buy flowers for the alter."

This is just one hypocrisy that I have found within my own faith, but I often see it elsewhere. Even though I was a devout alter boy, I soon became disenfranchised. I met some good men in the church, but overall the Catholic Church is about power and wealth.

Needless to say, I am wary of organized religion. My faith is in my heart where I worship and talk to God on a daily basis. Don't need a church or a priest for that. God answers me. I know what's right but I don't always do it. Still, I talk to Him. I trust God a lot more than any priest or preacher.

One of the best experiences Becky and I ever had was attending church at the Solid Rock Baptist Church up a hill in Southwest Roanoke. I admired Brother Perry, a preacher who never tried to convert me, but always supported my belief in Jesus. Members of the congregation were just as loving. One of them even came up to me after a service and said they were proud of me. "I always thought Catholics worshiped the devil."

Brother Perry was a true man of the cloth. Unlike Brother Larry, his talks inspired me to be a better Christian, to put my faith into practice, and to respect all forms of religion. Enough said about that, let me just say that each of us has a personal, inner relationship to forge with the Creator. Priests, ministers, and preachers can point the way, but we have to do the work ourselves. A congregation can be great support, which, I believe is the number one reason to join a church.

I wish you all the greatest of success. May you find peace with God. May your heart be filled with His grace.

Enough about that.

Daddy's funeral had a theme. "Jimmy knew the Shepherd, and the Shepherd knew him." It was repeated over and over, usually followed in song as the organ rose and the chorus began something like, "We're gonna take a little walk with Jesus."

Larry worked hard, sweat beading on his forehead, hands trembling and waving up to God, asking the Lord to take the poor soul of Jimmy Bland, bring him home and hold him close. Later I found out that the funeral had members from Larry's former congregation in the audience and he was trying to win some of them back. Whatever the reason, Larry did his absolute best and he created a memorable event.

We were not seated with the family. For some reason, Mary Jane and Brenda did not save us a place up front and we sat with Cherrie halfway back in the belly of the chapel. Even from there we could see Brenda jumping up, grabbing Daddy's cold corpsey hand and rubbing and kissing it, wailing like a professional griever.

I wept for Daddy that day. Didn't think I had that many tears in me. Ten years later my mother died and the tears came back, stronger and more subtle than before. They would sneak up on me and grab my heart. Death wounded me both times. This time he is closer still and I wonder if I will survive a third bout of tears.

The Bland Family: Brenda, Becky, Mary Jane, and Jimmy.

93

An unexpected event has made it necessary for Nick to return to Seattle. His landlady went crazy and evicted him (us, since we were living at his house too). I had paid the rent in advance before we left on this trip but she claimed it didn't happen. She was obviously too hell bent on getting us out of there to check her bank statements because my research proved otherwise. Being thousands of miles away with Becky in poor health did not phase her. We decided to capitulate, it was just not worth the fight. Life's too short, or so we thought, and God's justice is often harsh compared to our system of punishment. Just be warned if you ever decide to rent from a woman named Deanna on Whidbey Island, this was our experience.

Becky enjoyed our time on Whidbey Island. We lived there from December 2016 right up until we left on the bucket tour. Mornings were rough but we had a routine. Hot tea in the morning helped a lot. Usually she couldn't get moving until noon. Mostly she would lie in bed all morning.

Becky at Double Bluff Beach on Whidbey Island.

At the Meerkerk Gardens in April 2017, weeks before the Bucket Tour. Whidbey Island blooms with color at this time and, as you can tell, so does Becky.

I would take her on excursions, as we called them, to get her out of the house and living again. Whidbey Island is beautiful and it has many recreation and tourist sites. We visited every State and County Park, every City beach, and every town on the island. We went down dirt roads, parked at the beach at Ebey's Landing a lot, and ate dinner at different place every day.

These are two of my favorite pictures of her during these days.

These excursions were special. There were times I would have to pull off the road, park for a while and let her rest before continuing. On some days she was too weak to walk, but she would rest in the car while I went hiking.

We didn't know at the time that there was a cancer in her lower gut chewing away at her insides. It wasn't all excursions. We would take the ferry to the mainland often to visit her doctors. If her appointments were early, we would stay in a hotel in Bothell to make it easier. Nick would usually stay with us, accompanied by Duncan, close friend of the family.

One problem she had was an unusual growth on her chest. A strange red blotch appeared and it gradually got larger and more painful. She had trouble and some of her clothes would irritate it. Doctors eventually cut it off, and nobody ever said what it was.

In February, I took her for a test at Pacific Medical Center. The technician was getting ready to inject some dye in her for the test. He couldn't do it. She was too dehydrated. He did a lab test. Her creatinine levels were low and her kidneys were failing. I took her to downtown Seattle where they immediately admitted her to the hospital. Doctors installed stents to keep her urinary tract open. After five days of hospitalization I was glad to get her back home.

I must make note of another doctor who treated Becky, Doctor Katrina-Iiams Hauser, a Naturopath. She saw Becky through chemotherapy and had a large impact on her comfort. Her regular treatments of hydrotherapy and Craniosacral Therapy were a blessing.

Despite everything, we will miss Whidbey Island.

Airfare out of this part of the south is expensive, especially at the last minute. Nick manages to secure a flight out of Orlando which becomes our next destination. As we prepare to leave, Cherrie and Becky are sad. They had their girl time this afternoon, getting pedicures and eating sushi, but it wasn't enough. As we leave

Colombia Becky says, "Cherrie is my very best friend. She was there at all the important things. My weddings, Daddy's funeral, The good times and the bad times. Most of all, she knew the important things and didn't have to be told. That's a true friend."

Nick drives us towards Florida into the darkness and the thick, pouring rain. In the worst Seattle rain it never comes down like this. Nick has been working construction and likes to boast that they paint in the rain. Not sure it would work here. It is hard going, slow and tedious. Finally, we are all tired and Becky hurts so much that we have to stop on the north side of Jacksonville for the night.

Becky, Nick, Baby Berghita, and Duncan.

May 23

Nick's last day on the Bucket tour. I can't say enough about his help on this mission. He has been so supportive of his mother.

Unlike me, he is a natural caregiver. I know Becky will miss him. We talk about all the places we planned on visiting, the things we all wanted to do. Silly things and serious things: Dollywood, Itcheetucknee Springs, Unclaimed Baggage. My friend John in Neptune Beach was going to show him how to fix the struts on the car to stop it from rocking like a boat. It would cut down on Becky's car sickness for sure.

Anyway, in his honor, today is dedicated to three things on:

NICK'S BUCKET LIST

1 "If you're good, I'll take you on a tour of a major industrial facility." This is the promise I would make to Nick and Chris. Well, Chris mostly. Nick was really young. We're talking two or three, and Chris was in Middle School. Nick's too young to remember that I took him to see the Clydesdales when he was that little. Somewhere I have a picture of him petting one of the horses. I also have a picture of Chris mimicking his arm up the ass of a fiberglass replica of "Larry", one of the more famous Clydesdales. If you haven't figured it out yet, the major industrial facility is the Anheuser-Busch Brewery in Jacksonville and it really is an incredible industrial facility.

The first time I went to the Busch plant was when I worked for the Jacksonville Marine Institute in the late seventies. The Marine Institute took adjudicated youths and trained them in seamanship, marine biology, scuba diving, and ethics. They also had a program where students could work towards their GED and even get college credit. I ran the Young Adult Conservation Corps which hired people between the ages of sixteen and twenty three to work on various projects. These included coastal re-vegetation, marine fishery surveys, stone crab research, fish trap research, and helping with the construction of offshore artificial reefs.

The Busch Plant had a program on pride, a major part of their work ethic and their brewing process. It was a great program that focused on pride at every level. Let me be clear, this was the seventies and the pride I am talking about is not the type you see in the pride parade once a year. I'm talking bootstrap self evaluation and the benefits of being proud of yourself, your family, your community, and the work you do. It was an inspiration to the youth in our program.

Check out time at the hotel is noon and tours start at ten. Becky wants the extra time to rest. The hotel is on Dunn Avenue which becomes Bush Drive once it goes under the I-95 overpass. We are the first to sign in for a tour today.

The receptionist asks if we want a guide or do we want to proceed at our own pace. We choose the latter. She checks our identification and offers us a beer to take on the self guided tour. For Nick, seeing the plant brings back memories. We brew craft beer at home and to comprehend it on this level is truly impressive. Gone are the references to Spuds McKenzie, the party dog, and Bud Man, the super hero of the inebriated. Back in the seventies and eighties these were the icons of college students everywhere, myself included. Sadly, these cartoon celebrity sponsors were quietly retired, along with their counterparts like Joe Camel, an old R.J. Reynolds character that allegedly encouraged teen age smoking. Chris thought he was cool, wanted a Joe Camel jacket.

I used to remember more people on the bottling line, dozens of them, but it is super automated now. There are three of four guys walking around the lines, processing the defects kicked out by the machinery. You can watch this line forever, like a live version of *How It's Made*. The gift shop sells a personal keg, also labeled the world's biggest growler, a high tech device to keep beer fresh indefinitely. Nice gift for a beer lover. As we leave we pass a window and see lager tanks stretching into the distance. There are two men cleaning one out and we wave but they don't see us. We exit and look up from outside, realizing that there are four floors of these tanks built and supported by a framework of I-beams.

An impressive amount of beer. I wonder how much of it is drunk right here in Duval County.

2 Nick likes to explore his heritage. I'm not talking about his father's side, he knows enough about that! I can go back three generations on both sides of my tree and find peasants. One family historian told me that Delmedico was a corruption of Del Medici, meaning belonging to the DeMedici, and that we were once slaves of the DeMedici family. Don't know if it's true, but it sure would explain why we all like to work hard.

His mother's side is another story. Becky's Dad can trace his lineage back to Jim Bowie, and Becky's Mom was born, bred, and raised in the South. Daughter of the American Revolution. There's a reason why Becky puts her hand over her heart whenever she hears *Sweet Home Alabama*. Or why she can't resist singing along with *Freebird* every time it plays on the radio. The twang in her voice is another giveaway. People in Seattle love to talk to her just so they can hear that sweet cream and honey voice. Then there's the final cut, how she cooks Southern food.

Ask yourself who the fourteenth president was. If you answered Jefferson Davis, then you probably already know enough history to skip this section. Most every Southerner I know is still wrapped up in the Civil War, a conflict also known as The War of Northern Aggression. Nick likes to tickle his roots from time to time.

At the Hanging Rock Battlefield Trail in Salem, Virginia, there is a monument to Brigadier General John McCausland, a Southern War hero who, with the help of Confederate reinforcements under Jubal Early, stopped the Yankees at Roanoke and drove them all the way back to Lynchburg. Oddly enough, there is an impressive statue, not of McCausland, but of George Morgan Jones. George has no connection to the battle, he was just a philanthropist from Lynchburg.

I once took Nick to Front Royal, a center for Civil War re-enactments in Virginia. There are more battlefields and historic markers in the area than you can visit in a month of Sundays. You can buy every kind of Civil War item at the area gift shops. There is one more place we like to visit when we're in the area: *Dinosaur Land*. In our opinion it is the best dinosaur park. Their t-rex drips blood from its mouth, and everywhere there are beasts locked in combat. Plenty of photo ops. The fiberglass replicas are not your standard happy dinosaurs like you see at *Dinosaur World* in Cave City Kentucky or Plant City Florida, both of which we've visited. These dinosaurs look like they are popped out of the same fiberglass mold. *Dinosaur Land* is one of a kind.

Who collects dinosaur brochures? We do!

Side note: There is a strange attraction in Natural Bridge, Virginia called *Dinosaur Kingdom II*. Not your usual dinosaur park, this place is built on the premise that during the Civil War the North unleashed dinosaurs as weapons of mass destruction against the South. Giant replicas of Stonewall Jackson fighting a T-Rex, Abraham Lincoln keeping a pteranodon from eating the Gettysburg Address, etc. Goes down in my book as the most unusual dinosaur park.

Okay, back to the story: Nick's Southern Heritage. When we visited Cherrie yesterday we took time out to go downtown and walk around the capitol grounds. Lots of monuments, a parking garage and several buildings named after white people, an impressive statue of a mounted Civil War hero, monuments to the best American wars in the last three hundred years. And, oh, yes, a Black History Memorial. I wonder what South Carolina would be like today if African American men and women were allowed to contribute more to the growth of this state than picking cotton and rice, cooking, and such.

I might say here that Nick is not racist. He spent his early years on St. Thomas and he saw no color. In the second grade in Virginia he filled out a form and checked the box for black. He thought it had something to do with hair color or the fact that he was Italian. The teacher set him straight.

About an hour west of Jacksonville, off the Interstate and on Highway 90 is the Olustee Battlefield Historic State Park. This was the decisive battle for the State of Florida. The Confederate Army depended on food grown in this state. The North launched a series of blockades and secured northeast Florida. Union forces began to move in early 1864, landing en mass in Jacksonville. On February 15 they marched westward and were met by Southern troops. Outnumbered, the Southerners rallied and defeated the Yankees, driving them back to Jacksonville and pushing the war back to the coast of Florida. They secured the inland farms and the crucial supply of food for the Confederate Army.

The battle is re-enacted every year. Despite history, the Confederates always outnumber the Union troops. Face it, no one wants to be the Yankees. My friend Kerry Stratford participates in these events and he is in one of the pictures hanging in the museum. For a true Son of the South, there ain't nothin' better than playing soldier in a skirmish that we won.

Becky did not feel too good. She didn't even get out of the car to use the rest room.

3 Final stop: Ichetucknee Springs. This is a crystal clear river that comes out of the ground at seventy two degrees Fahrenheit. We used to tube down it during the hot Florida summers. Becky is not feeling well and won't be able to float down the river like she wants. Also, the tubing season does not open until Memorial Day weekend. That's when you can park in one spot and take a tram that runs between the beginning and the end of the tube run. It is raining but as we pull into the park it stops, long enough to hike to the Blue Hole and snorkel.

We are refreshed by the spring, our bodies renewed. Becky is rested, having slept while we played. Back on the road we drive hard for Orlando where a hotel by the airport waits for us.

May 24

We put Nick on a plane back to Seattle early in the morning. Becky does not have the energy to go to the airport and she says her goodbyes reluctantly. He promises to return if he can. His boss has been nice about letting him off work all this time. He has a lot to do including rent a storage unit and move everything to it.

Back at the hotel I bring her food from the breakfast bar. She eats a little, but mornings are hard on her. She takes nausea medication along with her pain meds. It's been a little more than a month on the road and I watch her health. The  push to get Nick to the airport is over. We can slow down now and travel at a slower pace.

I take her to the Goodwill Outlet in Orlando, one of her favorites. The prices per pound are cheaper than Seattle and she has found some of her favorite things here. She has a Tinkerbell sleep shirt that she has worn so much it looks like a rag. The clothes she has now fit loose on her. She is definitely losing weight. She is hungry afterwards. Using her phone she finds the menu of a Cuban restaurant in northeast Orlando that appeals to her. Once there, she eats like a pregnant woman.

May 27

Memorial Day Weekend in Florida and the beaches are packed. Becky and I are staying at Teresa's house. Becky is noticeably weaker. I take her to Waffle House for breakfast. She seems to eat a lot, but to me, anything over a mouthful or two or three is great (especially if it doesn't come back up). Usually I can save some portions and she will try to eat them later, small bites, a little bit at a time.

While we were in Colombia I heard her tell Cherrie that she is her own hospice nurse. I bring the subject up and ask Becky to tell me what a hospice nurse would tell me. She defers the question and says that when we get back to Seattle she will get me a real hospice nurse.

Being at Teresa's is refreshing. Becky and Teresa have a special friendship. They have been in each others lives for decades, meeting through me and the Debbies (Debbie Hullander, Debi Jarvis). Becky flew to Jacksonville in 2003 when Teresa had cancer and became a caregiver and nurse advocate for her. One of the great things about staying with Teresa is hearing Becky talk about God and religion with her. It is conversation I have been unable to provide.

Teresa and her husband Steven were at our 2006 Elvis wedding.

Sidebar: The night before the wedding the boys and girls split up for Bachelor/Bachelorette parties. I heard tales of their exploits, but as far as they knew we spent the evening at the Star Trek adventure over at the Las Vegas Hilton. Yeah, we did, but afterwards Eric wanted to check out topless dancing in Las Vegas. Nothing like a traditional bachelor party activity to get your testosterone level up.

A note about the Star Trek Experience at the Hilton: Awesome. It used a combination of live actors, technology, and special effects. First we were taken on a tour of a space station, but it was interrupted as we were attacked by Borg. We were collected, taken to what looked like a theater, and assimilated. I can still sense the creepy way they made you feel like you were getting Borg implants. The seats were animated and there were jets of air and things that happened around your neck. Fortunately, Voyager was nearby and we were rescued by Captain Janeway and her valiant crew. The Doctor used some miracle procedure to remove the implants and we were on our way...

To the next adventure. This time we were transported aboard the Enterprise. We stepped into a hotel elevator and after a few seconds the lights dimmed, you felt this tingle of air, and the walls shimmered. When the lights came on full we were in a larger room, a transporter chamber aboard the starship Enterprise. A uniformed security guard escorted us to the bridge where Captain Picard briefed us (via video). One of us in the elevator was his ancestor and the Enterprise had gone back in time to stop a renegade Klingon vessel from destroying the bloodline by killing his great, great, great... you get the picture. For our safety we were loaded on board a shuttle and as we took off, the Klingons appeared. There was a tremendous battle over Las Vegas in which the Enterprise prevailed. The shuttle crashed into the side of the hotel where a stunned maintenance man helped us get back to reality. All I can say is, I hope the wrinkle in time gets ironed out before my great, great, great, great.... You get the picture.

Tony made the comment that the ride was not your Disney simulator. He was right, as we were all a little shaken as we stumbled away from the wreckage of the shuttle.

On the way out we stopped at Quark's where they serve drinks that rival those on Deep Space Nine. A wide variety of drinks employed dry ice effects. I was tempted to try the Romulan Ale, but hey, that stuff's illegal. There was a unique drink dispenser behind the bar that, through some kind of strobe effect, appeared to draw liquid out of a glass. The bartender would put an empty glass in, hit a button, and it would flash. You would see drops of water falling upward. When the lights went out the glass was full. I'm still trying to figure out how they did that.

A note about the topless dancing: What happens in Vegas, stays in Vegas, or so we thought. Steven ratted us out the next morning. We couldn't squeeze anything out of the girls. They were pretty tight lipped about what they did and all I heard was "Dancing on the bar at Cowboy's."

Yeah. Right.

Becky and Cherrie all decked out for the Bachelorette Party.

June 1

I have been sick for a couple of days. Being sick has a counter effect to feeling bad. It raises your vibration, makes you more spiritual, or so that's what Lobsang Rampa says. But it also helps if you read spiritual stuff while you lay in bed. Reading helps me get back to sleep again when I wake up in the middle of the night. I'm reading *Edgar Cayce Story of Karma*, a book I got from Becky's Dad a long time ago. It turned up recently when we sold the house and I found it among our stuff.

James Bland was quite the man. I admired him a lot. Like I said before, he welcomed me to the family when Becky and I got married and told me to call him Daddy. My heart is bursting now just thinking of the power of his words and of all the discussions we had after that. He was a deep man and he shared that part of himself with me. He trusted me and loved me and was every bit a Father to me, a blessing to have for any man late in life. Now I have Daddy Frank, Mary Jane's new husband, but we haven't had the benefit of the time that Jimmy and I had together, but we're working on it.

Daddy and I discussed many things. He was a practicing Christian. *Jimmy knew the Shepherd and the Shepherd knew him.* Often times we talked about the Bible. Jimmy delved deep into Scripture, had a database of bible quotes and passages, all cross referenced and indexed. We talked about aliens, giants, Biblical quotes that supported all kinds of mysterious things, spring-boarding into other subjects. Which leads me to this book he gave me, one he wanted me to read, a wish I finally granted fifteen years after his death. If I only could have discussed this one with him.

June 3

There is an aspect of Hospice work that involves spiritual preparation and comfort for the patient. I have observed this through Becky's work. She has seen a diversity of religions prepare countless patients to meet their God and Creator for the unveiling of the last mystery. I wonder if I am providing any of that for Becky. She says she doesn't need it, and I believe her. I know from many conversations with her that she holds God close in her heart, that she is a true believer.

Are wise words a comfort or do they seem trite? Like most people in times of stress, platitudes come to mind, Bible quotes and sayings that only leave me empty and wondering. No one knows what lies beyond the veil. I can offer her no more comfort than a hollow priest with no bedside manner.

I face my own fears. Huddle in another room, press my fists into my eyes and hide what I cannot stop. Shivering like a child in the cold, I know her fears must be greater. There is not much I can do, it is in the Doctor's orders: "Hospice with focus on symptoms. Limit your trip to three weeks."

It has been over seven weeks. She is out against doctors orders. Her choice comes to mind, quality of life over quantity. Is chemo that bad of a deal? Trade four months for fourteen?

Would she be able to travel like this after chemotherapy?

The tour has made her happy, but I wonder about the additional stress. The back seat of a car is no substitute for a comfortable bed, no matter how many pillows and blankets you have. This car drives like an old boat. It needs work but it is the best we have in the Delmedico fleet. Becky uses pills to quell her nausea and we often stop for her.
She smiles through her pain. The time she has spent with loved ones and family members on this trip has been priceless, but she is paying the cost. It is hard to gauge the impact of travel, the stress of the road. How much can I attribute to that, and how much to the natural decline of her health? I have been watching a highly competent, compassionate woman grow into a child within a short period of time. I heard her joke with Cherrie, "I really am a dumb

blonde now, Honey. Not pretending anymore."

She spent a lifetime acquiring knowledge, applying it to the comfort of others. Now when she needs it, she has me, a clumsy, third rate caregiver that seems, at times, to irritate her more than help. I have no training. I work better with computers than with people.

I think I'm going to need that real hospice nurse long before we get back to Seattle.

Becky in her chemo hat.

June 7

Good news! Nick is returning to join us on the bucket tour. Things are progressing on schedule. He has help with the move and he found a vacant storage unit to rent. If all goes well he'll be here in a week.

I take Becky shopping at Goodwill. None of her clothes fit her anymore. When we began this trip she weighed a hundred and seventy eight. Now she weighs about one forty five, roughly a loss of twenty five percent of her body mass. She is less and less engaged in activity. The trip to Goodwill wears her out, nothing like she used to do. That woman could flat tear up a thrift store.

June 14

I picked up Nick at the airport around midnight last night. Becky found a condo to rent in Orlando and we have it for three nights. Since we're in Orlando, the vacation paradise, we decide it is time for something else on Becky's:

 # BUCKET LIST

Becky always wanted to go to Medieval Times. Nick bought the Father's Day Special so I get in free. We arrive early because we want to get a good seat but it doesn't matter that much. They let you into the castle but not into the arena, so you mull around in the shopping area while you wait. We buy a drink (two actually) and Becky gets liquored up on a few sips. It has been a long time since she imbibed and she is in good spirits for the tournament.

We cheer the red and yellow knight on to victory for a few fights, but over the course of the night he does not prevail. After eating, Becky does not feel well, but she insists that we stay and see the whole show. I can tell she is in pain and I forgot to bring her medicine with us, something I must remember to do from now on. These spells come and go and eating certain foods will cause Becky pain. It seems to be a constant five on the pain scale. I have heard her say she can't eat meat anymore and after observing her for a while I agree but this assessment is not one hundred percent consistent. As far as a source of protein, eggs in the morning seem to be all she can handle.

June 15

Nick wants one more shot at a theme park, his choice: Volcano Bay, a new water park at Universal. Normally we would go to Wet n Wild, our favorite place when we lived in Florida. Doctors said

111

playing in water would exercise Nick's legs and help him grow right. We took it to heart.

Wet n Wild in Orlando was awesome. Becky used to love sitting at a table in the kid's section where she could watch Little Nick play until he was tired. She made fun of the mothers that coddled their

children by positioning them in the tube at the top, meeting them at the bottom of the slide with customary applause, or (shudder) carrying their child's tube up to the top of the ride for them. She made Nick do all his own work.

Nick called this fun place "Gug-gug". When it was time to leave he would put on a horrible scene, crying, going limp in his mother's arms, yelling out for "Gug-gug!" People would look at us like we were beating the child. It's sad, but most of the time it was Becky holding him while I got the car to meet them at the front gate. Ten minutes down the road and he was usually sound asleep.

Alas, there is no more Gug-gug. As we approach Volcano Bay we see long lines. The report is in: Volcano Bay is at capacity, and it isn't even ten o'clock. We divert to Universal Studios.

We close down the park. Won't say much about the day, but when we leave Becky calls us. She is starving and hasn't eaten since breakfast. We left her money and menus of restaurants that deliver but she said she couldn't decide what to eat. I think in her muddied brain she couldn't figure it out. I reaffirm what I said before: she can't be left alone again.

June 18 – 22

 # BUCKET LIST

An incredible turn of events. Diana, a friend of our friend Sheree, is letting us stay at her condominium in south Jacksonville Beach for two or three weeks while she travels. It's on the third floor, higher than the sand dunes, looking out into the Atlantic. There is a pool down below and a private access to the beach.

It's Becky's dream come true: a bed that overlooks the ocean. Nick and I play in the waves every day. My friend Ric DeVere brings over a surfboard for Nick to try. Becky cooks meals when she has the energy, taking care of us as she always has. It makes her feel good and useful again. Her mornings are spent staring out at the waves in the Atlantic. The beach is a place where she grew up, an endless summer of life next to the ocean. She regrets it now, but she spent hours on the beach sunning and tanning. She really didn't tan that much, she is so fair skinned. She had bouts with skin cancer as well, but that is easily treated when compared to the kind of cancer that hides inside and feeds on whatever it can find.

There are not a lot of entries or writing these days, and I don't expect much in the near future. We're too busy having fun. Nick found a great sushi place and he often brings it home for Becky to eat. It seems to be something that will stay down and she loves the taste. She smiles a lot, especially when she is cooking, which is most every night. She starts with a full head of steam but she can fade at any time. Nick usually takes over for her. Under her tutelage he is becoming an excellent cook.

June 23

Becky is getting worse. She is sedentary, lying in the bed most of the day. Sometimes she moves to the couch to watch television with us, but that is the extent of it. Nick and I try to get her to go to the beach or join us in the pool but she is lethargic and does nothave the energy. She is exhausted after cooking and I can see it takes a toll on her, yet she insists on making dinner.

I lose my smile tonight. A combination of things come crashing down on me, leaving me empty of any joy. What remains is misery and sadness, hopelessness and immeasurable sadness. I am finding it difficult to summon the fake smile that I wear as a comfortable mask. It at least helped me support the illusion, deadening me to the reality of the situation.

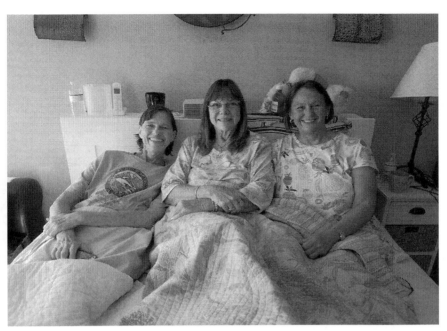

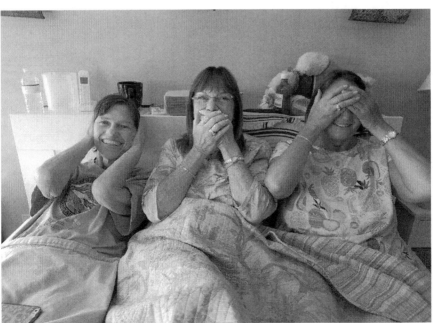

Becky, Teresa, and Sheree having fun at the condo.

She is in a lot of pain. The tramadol that she is taking does not seem to work any longer. She never wanted to take oxycodone but it has become necessary. I don't know how she lives with so much pain. She always indicates that it is in her lower abdomen.

Whatever is in there must be growing.

Diana has affirmations of faith taped around her house, little sayings and Bible quotes. They are a comfort and a source of strength. I wonder if she put them up for us, or for her own fortitude and faith. I know very little about her. Nick met her several times and he got all the instructions about the condo from her. What kind of person bestows a kindness of this magnitude on a stranger?

Someone who lives by the faith they practice. I wonder about Brother Larry's faith. I recall Jim and Tammy Baker, wealthy televangelists. In the end, I don't know. I am only responsible for my own faith. I forge my relationship with God in my heart, following my own path. It helps to read these affirmations and thank God and His mysterious ways.

This condo comes complete with a boogie board, party supplies, field glasses, and even a wonderful small dog named Kimora. Becky and Nick are in love with this dog. Me too. She loves to play fetch with a tennis ball and I love trying to trick her. She is smart and diligently searches for it as my fakes get better. I think we both enjoy this game because she gets so excited when she finds her tennis ball.

If only Becky had some of her energy.

June 24

The family surprises me with a birthday party. I turn sixty four tomorrow. Becky has contacted friends and they show up in droves. It's like a reunion. Lex, Rick Hightower, Kerry Stratford,

Joe Cox, Ric DeVere, my whole gang. We used to call ourselves
The Boys Club, a name I think Judy Pellerin gave us. When we
were young and dateless we would hang out together and do guy
stuff.

Like all clubs we matured. We all got into married or committed
relationships. Some of them survived, some didn't. Seeing my
friends again renews my strength. My smile has returned. My
friends offer their support and remind me that I am not alone.

The old time members also brought their kids, so Nick gets to hook up with the next generation. He gets invited to a party the next day so he can see how beach kids live and grow up.

July 1

Nick met a girl named Kim online and decided to go out with her. She is sweet, an accounting major at UNF[14], and obviously attracted to him. Becky is happy for him. She has been after that boy to get busy and provide her with grandchildren.

Becky tells me often that I need to move on after she dies. This conversation has been going on since her chemotherapy. I joke about a woman named Monica that she keeps telling me to find after her death. "She works at the Evergreen Hospice. You can't do any better than Monica." It has become a running joke. Fact is I can't do any better than Becky. Even in her illness she is a dedicated woman. I wish you were here to enjoy the dinner she just cooked.

July 8

We leave Diana's Beach Palace today, peace and memories swept away as we clean her condo. Becky hardly left the bed in the almost three weeks we've been here. We took her to Ellen's Kitchen in Neptune Beach one morning for the Surfer Special, but that was the only time she left the building. True to what she wanted to do, she prepared food and kept us fed and happy. Country fried steak, stuffed shells, manicotti, omelets, potato salad, chicken and dumplings, even Asian night, all followed by a Becky classic dessert like banana pudding or cake.

---

14 University of North Florida, my *alma mater*, known as yoU'll Never Finish in the day, but all that has changed now that it has evolved into a full time college. There was so much construction going on when I attended back in the late seventies that I suggested the school mascot be the Fighting Cranes. (construction cranes, not the birds.)

During our stay Nick and I manage to get the car fixed with the help of my friends. John and Nick put new struts on it, Mark changed the transmission fluid, and Jim Roe helped change the oil. We are ready for the road. First stop will be Teresa's for a night or two, then head out to Ichetucknee and on to Mississippi to visit my sister and my niece.

July 9

Change in plans.

Becky went into home care Hospice today. We headed out yesterday and made it as far as Teresa's house, barely fourteen miles from the condo. Bridesmaid Sharon came by for a visit and made an assessment and said it was time for hospice. Who am I to argue with a professional? And I am too close to the situation to admit it. Denial, as they say, is a powerful thing. I don't think I recognized the symptoms. I realized that I have been saying goodbye to her every day since February when she went into the hospital with renal failure.

It is a relief. The admissions nurse brings literature and comfort. Morphine is delivered by dark and Becky finally has the pain medicine she needs. I read a piece on caregivers and how they need to take care of themselves. I need that. Becky keeps asking me what I am going to do after...

I can't even write the words.

She thinks staying in Florida would be good for me. I have support here, friends that have offered me places to stay and recuperate. Anything I need.

Except her.

Hospice has allowed me to face that fact. I cannot change the inevitable, even when it comes to my own death. Acceptance. Just another horse on the Kubler-Ross[15] merry-go-round. Gotta love acceptance.

Like any normal married couple, Becky and I don't see eye to eye. I'm in acceptance, she lives in anger. Is there any middle ground, even in death?

We speak often and openly and intimately. She has vast clinical knowledge and she knows a lot about people and human psychology. Lying in bed and talking, she is my caregiver, helping me get on and off the merry-go-round, warning me of what comes next. Once I am settled, she quietly tells me her last wishes, how she wants to be cremated, how she does not want anyone to make a fuss over her.

July 12

Matt drove down from Tennessee once he heard his mother was in hospice. He brought Autumn and the baby. Becky's mother, Mary Jane, Frank and April also made the trip from Roanoke, arriving by plane the next day. Matt picks them up from the airport at the same time he drops Little Nick off. Nick must return to Seattle. They all meet at the airport and at least he gets to spend some time with his grandma.

Nick's boss[16] has asked him if he's ready to return to work. Becky and I discussed it with him and gave him the option of leaving. He has spent the best part of the bucket tour with his mother. He doesn't need to stay for the bitter end. He took the option and decided it was time to get back to his life. Sadly, when he says goodbye, Becky is delirious. She doesn't realize he is saying

---

15 In case you don't know, Elisabeth Kubler-Ross introduced the five stages of grief and dying in her 1969 book On Death and Dying. They are Fear, Denial, Anger, Bargaining, and Acceptance.

16 Bosses I should say. He works more than one job.

goodbye for good.

Smiles all around as the family gathers about Becky in support.

July 13

Family drama at the Seafood Kitchen. We all go out to eat. It is a long way to drive to the restaurant from Teresa's house, but Becky wants to dine there. The trip is hard on her.

Becky is mad that Brenda has shown up. She drove down from Roanoke and didn't travel with any of the family. Becky says her sister likes to draw attention to herself and is using her death to garner sympathy. I don't know if it's true, but the attention seeking is obvious.Brenda makes the statement several times that she does not eat seafood. The menu has an assortment of meat, including hamburgers and steaks, but Brenda makes a big point of ordering a lone baked potato. When it arrives, she prays over it like a mourner on a death vigil. Frank has already led us in a blessing so I ask her what she's doing.

Maybe the food tastes better if it is blessed twice.

From left to right: Brenda, Frank, Jane, Teresa hiding in the corner. Matt with Baby Victoria, Autumn, April, and Becky at the Seafood Kitchen.

Everyone else is happy with their selections. It's April's birthday, but nobody celebrates or brings it up. She sits quietly focused on her dinner. April loves crab and I watch her pick through a plate full of whole cooked blue crabs. Becky and I split a Captain's Platter consisting of shrimp, fish, scallops, deviled crab, cole slaw, and french fries. It was always her favorite.

Becky doesn't quite make it through the meal. She gets nauseous before the end. I comfort her but she is angry about something. April has a small trash basket that she is using for scrap crab shells. Becky wants to take it to the car and use in case she needs to throw up, which is highly likely. The waitress apologizes and says she can't take the basket and the restaurant needs to keep it.

Becky raises her voice, ranting about things, pointing out to people how I planted the sea oats on the beach. It doesn't even sound like her.

I help her up, stopping to assist her to the bathroom. She throws up and I tell her I will take her home. When we exit the bathroom, the waitress has the basket, a fresh bag lining it. "Please, take it," she says.

This the progression of the disease. Anger. It is not directed at anyone in particular. It is what is inside her these days, eating at her mind like the cancer is eating at her body. I do not fault her, only wonder how I would be feel, facing death.

July 14

It has been a week since we came to Teresa's, yet it feels like a year.

The family comes to dinner at Teresa's house. Teresa has gone camping with her new boyfriend over the weekend, leaving us alone in the house with the family. There is more family drama, and I won't go into details. I have heard Becky and her Hospice co-workers talk about the different ways families gather around the dying. Religion plays a key role, for it is the language we use to communicate with the Eternal.

There are some people who use the dying as some kind of sick badge to draw attention to themselves. It is obvious as they talk in a loud voice, strong enough to wake the dead. Loud is not good. This I know. Recently Becky told me to talk quietly and slowly, that her mind can't process too much at a time. I try to control myself and honor her wishes.

April helps me unwind after all the drama. We play Monopoly Deal and talk on the back porch for a while. She laughs when I tell her about a time when Becky was mad and threw breakfast across the lawn at me. I give her my take on Becky's life.

God sent her here to learn about Hospice from all sides. Becky has said time and again that Hospice was her calling. But first, she had to learn to care. Becoming a nurse was a part of that.

Before nursing she was a waitress. I first met her when she worked at the A&W on Beach Boulevard in Jacksonville Beach.[17] She

---

17 I lived on Williams Street and would ride my bike there to get a fresh root beer and a Teen Burger. She worked there. We never knew each other on a name basis and it was over a year later that Jay introduced me to her as his girlfriend. We never made the connection, uncovering this well into

always worked hard, something she learned from her mother. She worked a lot of food service jobs: Burger King, Ranch House, Red Lobster, and the GEE DUNK on the Mayport Naval Station.

While working for Red Lobster in Nashville Becky heard about a Title VIII Program to train as an LPN (Licensed Practical Nurse). It was tough getting in and she had to fight the bureaucracy as hard as she fought the wave of applicants competing for a limited number of slots.[18] It was a struggle, but she graduated from that program and went on to work at Vanderbilt. As an LPN she worked at many hospitals, just about every one in Jacksonville when she was an Agency Nurse for Nurse Finders. A lot of her early experience was in ICU (Intensive Care Unit) and the ER (Emergency Room).

In 1982-83 she was the Head Nurse at the Nursing Home side of the Kodiak Island Hospital. One day a canoe overturned with three people in it. The water off Kodiak is freezing, reaching into the mid fifties in the summer, cold enough to induce hypothermia. Two

_____

adulthood, something revealed during the thread of a quiet conversation.
18 The God Damn Tea story occurred while she was attending this program.

people stayed with the canoe while the other one swam to shore for help. He survived. By the time the other two made it to the hospital, they were in shock, body temperature below seventy degrees. They called Becky because no one in the ER knew how to use the Mark IV respirator.

Later, as I have told before, she studied with Cherrie in the Regents Program to become a Registered Nurse. She didn't have the ambition or the desire for a Bachelors in Nursing, said it led to more administration and less patient contact. While in Roanoke, shortly after her father passed away, she felt a calling.

"God told me to do hospice work." I have heard her say it many times. It wasn't long before she was working for Good Samaritan Hospice in Roanoke. Then, when we moved to Seattle, she worked for Evergreen at the Gene and Irene Wockner Center, gaining experience at a residential hospice. Her last job was doing home visits for Odyssey Hospice.

So, what I am getting at here is, her whole life flowed like a river, the source of it her caring nature. Her journey as a nurse fed upon that nature. At first it was for the living: Emergency Rooms and Intensive Care Units, Recovery Wards and Rehab Clinics. She got to travel and experience geriatric care in different cultures. She did private duty, home health visits, volunteer clinic work, almost every kind of nursing. She was exploring herself, finally arriving at hospice, her calling.

This present experience, this slow death, is about her learning it from the patient side. I believe that her work will continue beyond death. Maybe God has plans for her to work death from the other side, helping those who pass over. Seems like she'd like that. She used to call herself a *Death Nurse* every now and then. Either way, she's a restless soul and I don't see her sitting still for long, even in the afterlife.

I say goodbye to April. The family is leaving tomorrow. Becky is happy that the family drama will be over.

"Now I can get back to dying in peace," she says.

July 16

I talk to God too much these days, monopolizing His time with petty requests that resonate between "Take her and end her suffering" to "Give her time." Last night she wanted pizza and I ran out to get it, leaving her alone for the first time in a while. I was nervous, but when I came back with dinner she was happy. Ten inch supreme from Rubios that tasted just like an old school Nick's Pizza. It looked like her last meal the way she tore into it, but a lot of her meals look like the last, especially when she has a reaction to it. Not this time though. She ate almost a whole slice, picking at it in her usual fashion.

Afterwards she took another slew of pills and we laid in bed together and cried. She felt like everyone hated her, that the world had turned against her and that her life this weekend was derailed and full of misery, not just for her but for everyone around her. I admit the weekend went poorly, but she never asked for all these people to fuss over her. Indeed, her whole life was spent fussing over other people. All she wants right now is peace and quiet, visitors one at a time. Some people thought she needed a prayer circle, that it would bring her comfort and healing. I don't think it's the prayer that she's denying, just the way it's delivered. As her caregiver, I have to honor her wishes and tell people not fuss and pray around her.

I can't imagine how much pain she is in. To be eaten slowly, from the inside, memories dripping away while your mind stays active. I want to tell her that this is the world of illusion, the place of suffering, that her body will soon be made new again. I want to tell her that she will be with people that love her: her father Jimmy, Billy Love, Kathy Carver, her maid of honor Dottie, and our good friend Steven, beloved of Teresa. I want to hold her and hug her but she is fragile and I'm afraid I will break her and squeeze the life out of her.

July 17

Becky is bat-shit crazy today, talking and making no sense.

She woke up saying something about Steven telling us we were going skydiving. Then she was irritated that Nick was sitting on the sofa acting like Sheree Hullander, his legs crossed and rocking back and forth. Now she's asking me if I got the fish cleaned and put in the freezer. When I answer yes, she says, "Good, we'll have it for dinner." She goes into the kitchen and starts taking all kinds of things out of the cabinets until she finds the Hamburger Helper. She has trouble deciding which of the three varieties she wants. "Let's have a Gordon Ramsey cook-off with these," she says.

She jumps from one thing to the next. She wants to go to dinner, gets all dressed up, and then thinks she has to clean the house. I have heard her invite people over and tell them she will cook for them. This is one of those cases where the spirit is willing but the flesh is definitely weak.
The family dinner fiasco Friday was an example. Becky started the ball rolling and April and Autumn did their best to try and finish, but without Becky the preparation went way into overtime. And you can't teach Southern fry cooks how to prepare Italian food in an hour. Nick would have been good about picking up where she left off, but he is off the tour now.

What am I saying? The tour is at a standstill. Teresa has been the absolute best by letting us stay here.

The Hospice nurse, Jarrilyn comes by for a visit as does the chaplain. Becky unloads and tells him about the tension accumulated over the weekend with her family. She says that she has made peace with her sister and has nothing else to say about it. She says this is just a way for Brenda to draw attention to herself. "Boo hoo, my poor dying sister."

She complains about a bunch of people wanting to pray over her. "That's the last thing I want," she says. "But none of the family will honor my wishes."

"It's not their choice," says David, the chaplain.

"I don't think it's the prayer she's against," I say. "I don't think she'd mind if you led us in a prayer."

"No," says Becky.

David nods.

We pray after that, unselfish prayer. I just want God to shed some of His Light on Becky, bright enough so she could see his His hand enough to take it, be guided through the coming darkness and into the Light.

July 18

Yesterday, while the Chaplain and the Hospice Nurse were here, we spoke about the four most important things, a simple list of things that need to be said. They are: I love you. I forgive you. Please forgive me. Goodbye.

Simple, but powerful.

Becky and I sit in Teresa's Florida room. It is a peaceful setting, the intricate tile floor carefully laid and built by Steven. There are plants and overhead ceiling fans that help cool the soul. Just outside, the wind speaks to us in chimes, some deep, some feint and ethereal. It is the perfect setting.

I find that I can say only three out of four of the important things. I love her and I forgive her, and she forgives me. All the foolish things we did to each other. The arguments, the pain, the misshapen clay that made up our lives. We survived disasters, a hurricane and a water spout, termite swarms, and frozen winters in a tiny cabin outside Fairbanks. We survived each other.

But no one survives death. I find it hard to say goodbye. Especially when I have been saying goodbye to her every day for the past three months.

I tell her about what I have written in this book, about what I believe is the center point of her life. It has always been about caring for people. I think she learned that from GG, Lilian Bland, her father's mother. I begin to regurgitate all the things I wrote about

her career and her jobs, ending with how she landed in Hospice as a nurse, her calling. As her biographer, I want to get it correct. She does too, and she stops me from talking to clarify a fine point. It concerns a statement I have heard her say repeatedly: "God told me to work Hospice." The story unfolds.

It was sometime after Hurricane Marilyn, after we moved to Roanoke. By my reckoning it must have been spring of 2004. I turn on my recorder and capture her words. What follows is a loose transcript of what she says:

"This is something I've never told anyone before," she begins.

"I went to see *The Passion of the Christ*, that Mel Gibson film. I

130

sat in the car before going into the movie theater, thinking about my life, of what I was doing. Yes, there was caring but something was missing. There was happiness in sewing little girl's costumes for the school plays, cooking for the church dinners and leading the Sunshine Stretchers class. Raising Little Nick was a mission all unto itself, but there was no fulfillment. I watched people leaving the movie, the looks on their faces. I prayed to God to fill my life with something meaningful.

"I went to the movie. As I drove home the same thoughts consumed me. Where was the meaning in my life?

"I got home and turned on the television. There was a man on there talking about his life. He said it was meaningless and empty. He had tried to commit suicide. The only thing that stopped him was that he had three kids and couldn't find someone to take care of them. Deep in despair, he prayed to God to show him the path, to bring meaning back into his life. God told him to work hospice.

"At that moment I felt the presence of God in my life. I tingled from head to toe and I could feel God telling me to work hospice."

Even now, as she tells me this story, I feel something. My skin is tingling. I see now why she worked so hard, why she spent extra time with patients, why she never complained about the hours she put in after work, tirelessly entering data on the computer.

July 21

Bad day.

We got into an argument over her medications, but it was really about control. The problem is, she can't be trusted. Her memory is not well enough to remember what she does from minute to minute. Add to that hallucinations caused by pain medication. She takes morphine and atavan for pain and anxiety, metropolol for blood pressure, and compazine for nausea. When we go out I have more drugs in my pocket than a streetcorner dealer on a Saturday night.

I get angry. People have been asking me over and over, "How are you doing?", "Need any help?", and "If you need anything..."

My inner voice screams for release from this nightmare, but I put on a polite mask and say, "Thank you. No. I'm okay."

Debora Dier, an old friend of hers has come down from Seattle to sit with her. She and Teresa witness my explosion. They assure me she will be okay and tell me to take the day off. Thank goodness for friends.

The anger is directed outward but when I am alone in the car driving away it turns inward. How could I be so cruel? What kind of jerk screams at a dying old woman?

I drive away, down the street and aimlessly. I head east towards the beach, things bubbling in my head, a stew of muddy brain soup. I call the Hospice for help. They will have a social worker call me back. I try an online search for "caregiver support groups jacksonville" but get only a list of businesses, counselors, and assisted living homes. We fight for net neutrality but this is an example of the extreme. I become frustrated after several pages of links to money grubbing sites or blogs that point to money grubbing sites. I remember looking for caregiver support groups on Whidbey Island in Washington and being overwhelmed with the free support. There was even a State sponsored program that I started to attend specifically for caregivers.

I need help.

I drive by an old friend's house but I don't see his car out front. My heart sinks a little. I look as I drive by and I see his old lady on the front porch and pull in.

Cathy is an old soul. She quit her job to take care of her mother when she became ill. "There are human emotions, experiences we can sympathize with, but unless we ourselves go through them, we have no idea."

She uses an example. "I had friends tell me they were diagnosed with cancer and I felt all the pain and sympathy I could manage. But then one day I found a lump in my breast and I knew. In the two days that followed I knew exactly what it felt like."

"Now," she says patiently, the voice of a seasoned caregiver. "Put yourself in Becky's place." She lets that sink in a minute. "I know your life came to a stop when she got cancer, but hers did, too. She never asked for this."

It is good to have honest friends who pull no punches. You can only get truth from such a friend. I remember Becky once saying that, in the end, she always thought it would be her taking care of me, not the other way around.

The social worker calls and I get another dose. Jacksonville has a United Way helpline. Simply dial 211.

I have realized that when Nick was traveling with us, he not only shared the caregiving duties, but we also took time off together to decompress. We went to Universal, Ichetucknee, or just played in the surf. We took walks and shared experiences. Nick went home two weeks ago and I sure miss him. I've been taking care of her full time. I understand what Cathy is trying to tell me about experiencing a human emotion. I have trouble defining what I feel. It is difficult just trying to isolate the source of my feelings. Most of the time it is my own crap.

I believe in mindfulness and this is the most challenging environment to try to practice. But perhaps I am out of practice. It's an uphill struggle.

Hope is important because it can make the present moment less difficult to bear. If we believe that tomorrow will be better, we can bear a hardship today.

- Thich Nhat Hanh

July 22

 # TRIPLE BUCKET LIST

Becky has a remarkably good day, what I call a triple bucket day.

1 Becky loves to cook, and this morning she wants more than ever to make Debra Dier a farewell meal. She comes up with Eggs Benedict, which coincidentally is one of Debra's favorites. We are short a few ingredients, and she wants to go to Publix and pick them out herself. It is her first real experience in a wheelchair. I am able to pull a cart behind me while I push her. She keeps a basket on her lap and when it fills up I put the stuff in the cart and give her back the empty basket. There are times when she pulls the foot rests aside and moves around by herself. I can tell she is enjoying her freedom.

We go back to Teresa's house and she starts breakfast. There is fresh rosemary from the garden. Part way through she loses her spunk, but she completes the important things, the potatoes and Hollandaise sauce. Teresa finishes up, poaching the eggs. We have an elegant breakfast.

2 It has been over six months since I worked at Macy's and it was the last time Becky (or me or Nick) got any new clothes.

That in mind, we decide to go shopping. There isn't a Macy's at the Avenues Mall but there is a Belk's. I put Becky in her wheelchair again and push her past racks of discount merchandise. She is in her element. At the end of the shopping spree she has four or five outfits that she can't quite decide upon, and a stack of clothes on the dressing room floor as large as any pile of autumn leaves.

3   We get all dressed up in our new clothes and go out to dinner at a fancy restaurant, something Becky has wanted to do for a while. She wants to go somewhere that has linen tablecloths and napkins and more than one fork. Our shopping spree lasted a while and it is a late dinner. We dine at the Tree Steak House in Mandarin, a place we had gone to as young adults. They do not have the salad bar anymore like they used to. The original owner retired and the new owners decided against the bar. It is still good. Becky eats half a bowl of onion soup, a wedge salad, and digs into her meal of pork tenderloin and Parmesan encrusted risotto.

I am amazed she has the energy for all this activity. Overall it was a banner day that I can only describe as a Triple Bucket day.

July 23

Bad day. Depression has set in. Becky knows what is happening to her and it comes crashing down on her like an avalanche. She apologizes for being a burden. She cries a lot, hiding behind closed doors in the back bedroom. She is in pain, emotional and physical, and she does not want to be disturbed.

July 24

This is a fretful day, a confrontation with reality. Becky asks me, "Will I die today?"

"I don't know, Honey," I reply.

135

"It better not be in the next three days," she says. "God wouldn't do that to me."

Tomorrow is Nick's Birthday and the day after is Matt's.

"I'm worried about what I can't remember," she says. "I can't remember what I'm worried about but I know it's something I really need to worry about."

"It's okay," I say. "Don't worry about the big things. Or the small ones. I can worry enough for the both of us."

"That's the problem, you don't know what to worry about," she says. "You don't know the difference between the big things and the small ones. You'll worry about the wrong things."

"I'll try to keep it straight," I say.

I know what to worry about. She told me about a new lump in her throat, something that pinches against her esophagus, making it difficult to swallow at times. Then there is a mysterious cut in the back of her head that she doesn't know how she got. I look at it and it's an ugly scab. We clean it up and do what we can but it still smells bad. She told the nurse last visit that she fell and I remember her slipping in the kitchen. The floor was dry but try telling her that. She makes slight of the symptoms but I know what to worry about.

What is the world like when you forget what you did a few minutes ago, if you can't remember yesterday, or your mind can't figure out a card game you once played with childish glee? What is it like to feel lost, not even remembering what you were worried about?

There is silence for a while. The wind blows the chimes outside Teresa's Florida room.

"Sometimes, I blame you for my cancer," she says. "I know that's not true, but I want you to know that it's just anger. It's not true."

I know. Anger is one of the Kubler-Ross stages. I worked through denial months ago. I live in acceptance, continue to say goodbye to her every day. Keep a sober face when she asks, "Am I going to die today?" I learned long ago not to bargain with God, although Becky's struggle makes me think about my own life, and death of course. That leaves fear.

I can feel her fear at times. It manifests as cold. I can hold her tight, spreading my warmth to her through close embrace, but it is still there. She trembles and no amount of warmth will push back the fear. It goes away after a time, and she will turn and whisper, "I love you."

Is this the last time I will hold you? She has told me before that most hospice patients die at five in the morning. She says it might be because that's the time they do rounds in nursing homes.

July 25

She wakes me up at 4:00 AM. Anxiety, pain, general discomfort. I give her medicine and lay in bed, hold her close and pet her. Comfort, a gentle touch that sends a message to the mind, better than words, I think.

So many regrets pour out of her mouth. I listen to a litany of self defamation, pain directed inward, born of lost confusion or desperate confession, I don't know what, some kind of emotion I am trying to understand.

God help her.

I take her out to Stein Mart, another of her favorite stores. She wants to buy a dress for a ceremony we have been talking about.

She also needs new underwear. She keeps losing weight and there's not much I can do about it.

I like her in the Ralph Lauren, myself.

She tries on clothes and I give her my opinion and snap pictures. After trying on many outfits she has found the one she wants.

The perfect outfit! Now all we need to do is find a shoe store.

July 27

Today we are both having a bad day. My foot is swollen and Becky is taking care of me. It's working, the swelling has gone down enough to ease the pain. I can limp around better than yesterday.

Becky decides she wants to host a dinner party. Hard to deny a dying woman any request, but I go to the store and bring back the ingredients for stuffed shells, spaghetti, and salad with beets. She invites Jim Roe and Cathy (a.k.a. "Baby") come over tomorrow. We start preliminary food prep around 2:30 and barely get through at 6:00 PM. It is hard for her doing things in spurts. Also her mind isn't quite working right. She boils water and forgets why she is doing it. We sit down for a break and she turns and looks at me stone cold and says, "Did you order the pizza?"

I remind her that she is cooking a fantastic meal and she asks, "So, how many people are coming over tonight? Eight?"

She is child like, smiling goofy at times, and then she is comatose, nodding off, her eyelids closed, her breathing shallow and forced.

Is it the progression of the disease or drugs? Probably both, but what do I know, I'm a layman, and I don't know squat about dying. But I'm learning. My friend Mark calls, checking in to see how we are doing. After the report he sheds some light. He had a wife die of breast cancer.

"It's different than a divorce," he says. "Completely different emotion."

Having divorced Becky I answer, "I know what that's like."

"You'll be numb from the death, but the next morning when you wake up alone, and you realize it, there's no description for that emotion."

I have an emotion now that I can't decipher. Closest thing might be knowing you are about to be in an accident, a bad one, unable to prevent what comes, staring in shock as the horror unfolds, waiting with shallow breath for the final outcome, life or death.

July 28

I wake to the sound of coughing and retching. Becky is in the bathroom. It is five AM.

I calm her, give her morphine and atavan, a hot cup of tea followed by a cold cup, then a glass of ice water. Her breathing is deep and rapid. I hold her like it's the last time, petting her for comfort. Should I call hospice?

Hours later she thanks me, saying whatever I did helped a lot. She is past whatever fit held her in its grips. I move her to the sofa, feed the cat who is mewling loudly for her food, clean the bathroom and replace the bags and clean the two buckets she has soiled. The water in the toilet is dark and bloodstained.

Despite her bad health she has her dinner party, preparing food that evening for our friends Jim and Cathy, We have appetizers, salad, pasta and stuffed shells with garlic bread and a dessert made of cake and berries and fresh whipped cream. It is fantastic, probably her last dinner party.

July 29

I take her to visit Bridesmaid today. A terrible thing has happened. Sharon went into the hospital two weeks ago complaining of back pains. After examination the doctors determined it was pneumonia and admitted her immediately.

They gave her medication and she had a reaction to it, a bad one. She slipped into a coma and had to be put on life sustaining measures. For days she lay in the hospital on a ventilator while her children hovered close by.

The effect on Becky was devastating. She began to panic, began to imagine conversations with Sharon, even said at one point that she thought they were going to die at the same time.

Miraculously, Bridesmaid survives.

I take Becky to see her. She is staying with her daughter Angie here in Jacksonville. It is a bittersweet reunion, the two old friends looking all the more rough for the recent treatment. Sharon notices immediately that Becky's left leg is swollen. Sharon also examines the wound on Becky's head. The scab lies deep in her hair and behind her ear. It has grown larger and has leaked pus for a day or so. I keep telling her to stop picking at it.

Once again I find my layman skills lacking.

July 30

Becky wakes up early again today. Her right eye is swollen so much that she can barely see out of it. It is Sunday. I call hospice and they immediately tell me they are sending out a nurse. I am relieved, but we are not out of the woods yet.

"I'm going to die today," she tells Teresa.

"You can't," says Teresa. "Today is my birthday. You weren't going to die on Nick's birthday or Matt's, and you're certainly not going to die on my birthday."

The hospice nurse, Shannon, arrives and examines her. Community Hospice is an excellent group and I listen carefully to the conversation between her and Becky. Shannon begins to tell Becky what to expect next in the progression of her care.

"I know what's coming," says Becky.

"She was a Hospice nurse at Evergreen in Seattle," I say. "Fifteen years."

"It's dreadful knowing what's going to happen next," says Becky.

Shannon does all she can to keep her eyes free of tears, but it is hard. Becky starts to cry, too.

"I'm going to be that patient that screams and rips all their clothes off," says Becky. Shannon laughs for a minute, but the sudden, dreadful change in her expression tells me that it is a real possibility, a symptom of her dementia.

As I listen to them talk about what will possibly come, it is all I can do to sit there. Becky knows what is happening to her and there is nothing I can do about it. I can make her as comfortable as possible but I can never take away her pain and suffering. The morphine may be able to, but then what about that knowledge? Why can't that part of her memory go away?

"Can you check something else out for me?" she asks.

Her head is oozing pus and Shannon examines that as well. It smells foul and Becky says it gags her sometimes. Shannon talks with a doctor over the phone and an antibiotic is prescribed. "Medicated shampoo would help, too," she says. Becky and Shannon continue talking for a bit. I leave the room.

The drugs come that afternoon and we start treatment immediately. I face a new terror now. Facing death is one thing, facing it with courage is another. I have a new respect for Becky.

July 31 – August 1

Cherrie arrives today and Becky is excited. She is staying at Teresa's Hospice/Hotel tonight and then the Queen Bees are heading to the Courtyard at Jacksonville Beach tomorrow for some friend time.

It is good to see Cherrie here. In the first half hour she does a patient assessment on Becky. There are tiny black spots beginning to appear on her hands. The wound on her head is spreading and it smells worse despite the medicated shampoo. Becky picks at it and it must itch like crazy.

Please stop picking at it.

144

I take her to the hotel. Cherrie goes on ahead to take care of all the administrative chores, renting the room, getting her stuff settled, and checking out the venue. Becky is weak and I use the wheelchair to transport her. She seems to accept this, but I know she never would have wished for it. She and Cherrie took care of a quadriplegic. Becky once sat for a man with ALS. A wheelchair is the last thing she wants, but it is a necessary way to help her get around.

The last time she was in a wheelchair was 1981. We lived in Kodiak and for fun we would climb the mountains on the island. One time we climbed Barometer Mountain near the airport and she hurt herself on the way down. She sprained her ankle and had to painfully make her way down the mountain on her butt.

She wanted to go to the salmon festival that weekend. It had been something she looked forward to. God, she was in such pain. Hobbling around on a broken foot for three days in denial. Yes, at work she found out it was not a sprain, but a broken foot. Her friends at the hospital set it and put a cast on it. (Health care was not as problematic back then as it is now, especially in rural Alaska.) The salmon festival was out. Too much walking.

Or was it? I borrowed a wheel chair from the hospital for the day and took her there. I remember her feasting on salmon, her wheelchair pulled up to a table. I wheeled her through the crowd, she loved people watching. A man came up to her and said, "You look like a lady who needs a balloon," and he tied a helium balloon to her wheelchair.

That was the last time she was in a wheelchair. This time it is different. She is weak. She would never have wanted to use it unless it was absolutely necessary. During her chemotherapy I tried to get her to use the motorized chairs that stores have at the entrance, but she refused.

We arrive at the hotel and Cherrie has a room overlooking the pool and the ocean. They are all smiles as they settle in together.

145

I leave her in Cherrie's hands. She bought them each a shirt saying "Queen Bee." Life is good again.

August 3

I am watching the progression of this disease. She looks like a stick figure, she has lost so much weight. She has no continuity in her life. This morning we go to breakfast with Teresa and her friends Michael and Angie. She and Teresa split a mushroom, spinach and cheese omelet that she wants so badly. When it comes, she doesn't remember ordering it. It doesn't matter, she can't eat much of it anyway.

There are days she has the energy for some activity, but most of the time she lies in bed or on the couch. Her nurse comes to visit often, Jarrilyn. She is a big, smiling woman and she and Becky have bonded. She tells me later, "Jarrilyn is the best hospice nurse. She's everything I need, a blessing at this time in my life."

I agree with her. Her nurse has gone beyond the norm. They talk about hospice work like old friends. "When is the last time you took a lunch?"

"What's that?" says Jarrilyn. "You mean when I sit and code on the computer while I stuff something down."

"They tell you to take that break in the office," says Becky.

"They don't know what they're talking about."

Becky explains to Jarrilyn that she is involved in a class action suit against Evergreen Hospital, an attempt to get paid for all the hours she worked through lunch.

"Don't think I'm going to do something like that," says Jarrilyn. "I'll just keep working through my lunch when I need to."

Jarrilyn is dedicated. She spends more time than she has, biting into her busy schedule and taking up her precious time. I know what it's like. Becky started having problems before she was diagnosed with cancer. She was worried so I drove her to visit patients. I waited in the car for hours sometimes. Now I know what went on. The time Becky spent with her patients was now being paid back to her in triplicate, thanks to Jarrilyn.

The word gets around that Becky was a hospice nurse, there seems to be extra effort. Almost like Community Hospice is taking care of one of their own. They order massages and visits from social workers and chaplains. Her doctor comes on a home visit and she is wonderful. She brings Becky some of her honey, natural and fresh, made by bees from pollen in coastal flowers. It makes her

147

honey all the sweeter. As I prepare her tea I imagine that I am adding all that love and consideration.

Becky trying to take a selfie so she can see the scab on her head.

August 6

I take Becky shopping again. I can tell by her enthusiasm that she is one hundred percent behind it. She is so engaged in this activity. We start at Michael's, she's been looking for accessories. Something to go with this white dress she bought at Stein Mart last week. She has this basic ensemble, a white dress and a top, something that she is going to wear for a Ceremony we are planning soon.

She is not doing so well. The scab on the top of her head is getting bigger. It doesn't smell bad anymore but she keeps picking at it and it is getting worse.

"Stop picking at it," I say.

"I'm NOT picking!" comes the answer.

Lord, give me the strength to accept the things I cannot change...

August 7

Caregiver fatigue.

Becky tells me that she wants me to die with her, that she can not take this journey alone. I tell her that I have more to live for, that I have unaccomplished goals and dreams I still harbor for myself. I remind her that she will soon be with friends, people she has missed like her Daddy, Rod and Mary, and her old friend Kathy Carver. I tell her I will be along soon enough.

The road is getting rougher. This morning I feel like I want to die and end this nightmare. I sit and meditate, do some yoga but the awful truth remains. I feel better, but then I think of what it must be like for her. I rededicate myself to caring for her, a promise I made to her forty years ago.

I recall the Beatles song that played when I made the vow. We lived in a tiny one room apartment in Atlantic Beach. If you weren't careful you could easily hit your head on the loft bed. How we both fit in it to begin with was a testament to love. We took the art of cuddling to a new level.

When I'm Sixty-four was playing and we were singing along. When you're twenty seven you feel immortal. Becky had not yet faced cancer. Her life consisted of spending summer with one boyfriend in Alaska, then coming to Florida to winter with me. *Will you still need me, will you still feed me, when I'm sixty-four?*

And hence the promise was made. It was easy. Even though we weren't married, I knew she was already my best friend, my confidante, my love.

Keeping the promise is another thing. Some days I am not taking care of Becky, only the shell of a human, a suffering zombie who cannot remember that they were once a beautiful being, an angel of mercy, dedicated to relieving the suffering of humanity.

I will say this. Love, true love, sustains us. It allows us to do tasks that would otherwise seem insurmountable. It heals the hurts, and the pain and suffering. When she looks at me in lucid moments and smiles, her lips pursed in a kiss, and she whispers "I love you," in a hoarse and soft voice, I know I have the strength to continue on and see this through to the end.

She is restless. I wake up this morning to find she has packed everything in the room during the night. "I'm ready to move," she says.

There are other signs that her mental capacity is declining. "When did April leave?" she asks. I gently tell her that April isn't here. Now she asks, "Where did Nick go?"

Sometimes she alerts me to things. "There are people running around the house." It's dark and I go outside and check it out.

"Only cats," I say, but part of me wonders if she *did* see something. There are times she looks at me and thinks I am Teresa, Little Nick, or someone else. I have had conversations with her where she refers to me in third person. I was going to the store yesterday and asked her if she needed anything.

She said, "Italian ices. The good ones. I don't like the cheap ones he buys."

August 8

I take her to see Doctor Revollo about the strange growth on her head. The whole left side of her scalp is infected with some kind of brown scab. She has scratched it repeatedly and exacerbated the problem, even to the point of pulling her hair out. Now it has spread and will require a doctor's treatment.

Jaime Revollo is her old doctor. She met him at St. Vincent's in Jacksonville when she worked there. She saw his caring manner with his patients. "I want him to be my Doctor," she said. She made it happen.

Doctor Revollo saw her through her first cancer. He saw her through the birth of Little Nick. We went to the Florida Keys on assignment for Florida SCUBA News. Her water broke, but she didn't know she was a few months pregnant at the time. She thought it was ovarian cysts. He did a pre-surgical sonogram.

"I've got good news and bad news, depending on how you look at it," he told her. "It's not cancer, it's a fetus. You're going to have a baby."

It has been twenty years since we've seen him.

It is very revealing, what a patient will tell their doctor and not their spouse. I'm sitting in the corner and he asks her, "What can I do for you today?"

"I think I've had a stroke," she says.

It suddenly makes sense to me. The loss of memory, the slurred speech. I study her carefully and notice, as if for the first time, the droop on the right side of her face.

"I have tremors," she says. "Seizures."

"What about the wound on your scalp?" I say to her, reminding her of the main reason she is here.

"Oh, yeah."

He examines it, knows just what it is. He prescribes shampoo. He also gives her gabapentin for her seizures and tremors.

As we leave the doctor's office I am hopeful. She's going to get better.

August 10

Today is a special day, one we both have been looking forward to. Becky enjoys a Krystal for breakfast and we get off to a good start. She has packed and I lug everything out to the car. The wheelchair is in the trunk and I squeeze as much as I can on top of it. The back seat is also full and I ask Becky if we really need all this stuff.

"Yes, we do," she says.

I go back to the task at hand, taking a load of hanging clothes to the car.

I am spending less time writing and more time taking care of Becky. She is noticeably weaker and there are more signs that her health is failing. She has tremors and long periods of senility. There are times I believe I am talking to an empty vessel, sometimes it is an innocent child, sometimes an angry wife. Always it is a frail old lady with no recollection of her past.

She doesn't ask a lot of questions like she used to. She complains about the lump that is growing in her throat. The growth on her head must itch constantly. I try to keep her from touching it but it is difficult.

The bucket list has dwindled. I don't think she has the energy for anything. We've been talking about doing this for a week now and the time has finally come.

BUCKET LIST

We dub it The Last Romance, a second and final honeymoon. It comes out of the planning for the bereavement ceremony, except we decide, since it is an undoing, to do it in reverse: the honeymoon first and then say our goodbyes.

We spend two nights at the fabulous Howard Johnson's in the heart of the St. Augustine historic district. The street behind it is Becky's favorite. It is lined with trees that hang over the road, dripping with Spanish moss. The Fountain of Youth is on one side, its weathered coquina wall adding a venerable sense of age to the street. You can almost hear the whispers from the past. The HoJo has a tree on their property commemorated with a placard that says it is six hundred years old.

Which is about how old Becky feels. The honeymoon is hard on her. The first day is okay. We have lunch at an outdoor bistro and share shrimp tacos and a wedge salad. Then we check into the hotel. Becky has packed everything and I mean EVERYTHING. I think she thought we were traveling again.

It comes in handy. We have fun. There is a brief fashion show as she tries on different outfits, modeling them runway style, deciding what to wear for dinner. It is tiring for her, and after a quiet rest we have a late dinner at Ruby Tuesdays. I can not believe the plate she brings back from the salad bar.

They advertise sixty six items and I think she has one of each crammed on that plate. She is slow and careful, keeping it level so nothing will fall off. I see a couple of people glance at her, this frail old lady shuffling back to her seat with a plate ten times bigger than her stomach. On the plus side, she picks at it until she gets dizzy, weak, and nauseous. I slide into the booth beside her and hold her, petting her, stroking her hand like it is our first honeymoon. I pay the check and get the dinner to go. They let her take the leftover salad.

So ends the Last Supper. I sit in the hotel room and edit and format this book. There is a sense of urgency to my actions and I try to stay focused. It gives me something to do.

Tonight I am on the edge with her.

I watch television, work on the book. She wakes up and she is weak. I help her get to the bathroom. I feed her some of the leftover dinner, cutting small pieces of chicken, bringing them to her mouth and, like a toddler, telling her to open wide. She smiles, child-like, and tells me she loves me. It's a beautiful thought to sleep on and I wipe her mouth, give her bedtime medicine, and ease her gently back on the pillows. Love is the sustaining thing I live on right now. It is the heart and the energy that helps me when I need to bathe her or take her somewhere or comfort her.

Becky at the Bistro on our Last Romance.

August 11

I wake the next morning, try to roust her but she is in a deep sleep. I go to the breakfast bar and eat, bring a few things back for her. She is still sleeping.

Lunch time approaches. I eat the breakfast I brought for her, nibble at last night's leftovers. I take a short walk, afraid to leave for any length of time. When I return she is awake.

"Ready for some honeymoon activities?" I ask.

She nods, a smile as broad as any I have seen in the last month.

"Let's get ready," I say.

After a long, rough morning we finally make it downtown for some sightseeing. I put Becky in her wheelchair and push her through the old quarter. The cobblestone and brick streets are hard and we move slow and easy. In and out of stores we go, a stop for gelato, a cruise through a clothing store. She can't resist the bling and at a jewelry store I plunk down a small wad of cash thinking that the smile on her face is priceless. My heart is breaking as I hook a necklace behind her fragile neck. Her head is permanently bent forward and it is an effort to keep her head up and look at everything. Her spine has realigned itself to be comfortable backed and braced by pillows, osteoporosis taken to an extreme.

Her hand touches the necklace, her fingers rustling through the tentacles of chain. There's that million dollar smile again. She turns to me and says something but I can't hear her. She speaks in a whisper and there is too much background noise.

After a few hours she is exhausted, leaning sideways in the chair. We go back to the hotel. It is a little after five and she sleeps all night. Dinner and dancing are far from both of our minds.

157

August 12

Final day of the honeymoon. Up at seven. A trip to the breakfast bar, a bath, morning meds and she is ready.

Two bites of bagel, a spoonful of scrambled egg, and a piece of sausage and she is back to sleep. I pack and load the car, then wake her at check out time. We are close to Sharon's, about an hour away, and she wants to visit Bridesmaid one more time. They have both been through a lot lately.

She sleeps the whole way, awake enough for a stop in Titusville at the Moonlight Drive In. Two bites of a chili slaw dog and she is back asleep. On to Bridesmaid's where she asks to lie down and sleeps the whole visit. Sharon gives me a nursing assessment. "You should consider a residential hospice," she says.

I tell Sharon I will call hospice tomorrow morning. She and Angie help me load Becky in the car. Becky can hardly walk. I drive her back to Teresa's in silence.

August 13

I call the Hospice hot line today. Her decline, even in the last twenty four hours, continues to be significant. She is weak and senile. I have been using a potty next to the bed for her. I moved it out of the way before she went to sleep, took the pot out and cleaned it. I placed everything on the handicapped shower seat in the bathroom to dry.

I woke up in the middle of the night to find her seated on top of the pottyware, balanced on an upside down bowl on top of the guide ring on top of a shower stool. She had peed on it all. I gently helped her back to bed where I found a wet spot. I put a towel over it and moved her to the fresh side of the bed.

When I wake up this morning she is on the toilet. How she managed to make her way from the bedroom to the bathroom is amazing. I help her up and move her to the couch so I can wash the sheets. I wonder how long she had been stuck there, sitting on the toilet, unable to get up.

The hospice hot line answers and puts me through to triage. A series of questions and they decide to dispatch a nurse. While I wait for them I watch her sleep, her breath uneven, sounds that I have never heard coming out of her mouth. A thought passes through my mind. I have been able to face three out of four of the cornerstones of hospice: I love you, I forgive you, please forgive me, _____?

I won't say it out loud, but it builds within me, like the tears that I will not let out.

I pick up a piece of paper, her med chart, and begin scribbling on the back of it. I look at her again, pace for a minute, blow my nose and dry my eyes. I scribble some more and a poem springs from my heart:

The Goodbye

Remember my dear, remember my dear,
    We've both been here before
Remember my sweet, close to your death
    Beyond us lies so much more
The pain is over, the sadness ended
    The crippled body gone
A new one waits, God's next creation
    Life *does* go on and on
So rest my sweet, I'll hold your hand
    And send you on your way
I'll see you later, don't wait for me
    I'll be home at the end of my day

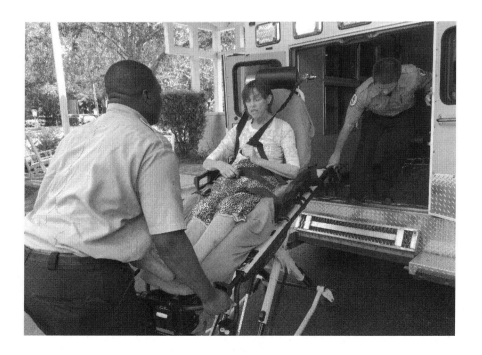

When she arrives the nurse makes an on site assessment. It is time. An ambulance arrives a short time later to transport her to the residential hospice. She is delirious, telling the EMT's that they will get a pin for this. I follow in the car and tag along as they process her at Community Hospice. There is no red tape and she is in bed and asleep before long.

I man the window seat and thus begins my vigil. There is a man outside the window, bent across a railing, staring into the empty depths of a pond. I hear crying down the hall, I hear sounds of comfort. She talked about opening a hospice at one time.[19] In her best imagination this is what she envisioned. She is at the end of the hall overlooking a lake. A plume of water sprays into the air. I see rainbows in the mists and there are trees and shrubs lining the lake. It is a peaceful place to be.

I hang around all day, feeding her and helping her while she is awake. It is never more than ten or fifteen minutes and she slips back into a deep sleep afterwards. The day is long and I sit in the corner and work on this book. Teresa comes for a visit. I sit and mope, listening to Becky's gargled breathing until I realize I am exhausted. The house is five minutes away and before the clock strikes ten I am joining her in slumber.

August 14

A stream of visitors and phone calls all day. Sheree came first, bringing coffee and comfort. Angie and Audra, Bridesmaid's daughters, both came by to see her, one in the morning, one at night. Audra brought her baby, Sierra. It was the perkiest I've seen Becky in a while, rivaling the excitement she gets when Nick calls. He called later, of course. He calls her practically every day.

---

19 She had a plan to build it in the guise of an adult family home. We attended classes and were remodeling our home just before she was diagnosed and started chemo.

During a brief lucid moment I manage to get her on the phone with her mother. The moment is fleeting and after a minute she begins slurring her words and snoring.

Sleep, my love. You need rest.

August 15

A harpist entertains us here in the room. She just came in with a stool and the instrument and set up. What a treat! As she plucks some strings and warms up I speak with her. "She's out, fast asleep. I doubt she'll hear it but I will."

"She'll hear it," she says. "The sounds penetrate the body, she will feel the vibration"

She plays Amazing Grace. Becky is somewhere between sleep and waking but as she plays I stroke her hair gently. I can see water gather in the corner of her eye. It was her Daddy's favorite song.

Jarrilyn comes to visit her. She tries to rally Becky. She is awake but she does not recognize her hospice nurse. Jarrilyn says goodbye to Miss Becky. I give her the original copy of my poem, *The Goodbye*. Jarilyn explains that she has a collection of poems from her patients and their loved ones. I was honored to contribute to her collection.

I can already feel the emptiness. A preview of what it will be like after she's gone.

I have been carrying her cell phone around along with a bag of her stuff. The phone has been on the whole time. It's no longer needed, she cannot answer it and I doubt the caller would understand her. Her speech has become difficult, barely audible and garbled. In addition to losing her mind and her memory, she has now lost the ability to communicate clearly. She lies in bed and snores, a raspy sound that sometimes echoes a croaking frog.

I am visited by a Psycosocial Specialist. I don't know what that is, and it prompts a fun game with my friends as I ask them "What's your corporate title?"

But it is all part of the excellent service here at Community Hospice. Becky would be proud of them and say the same. She might have even worked for them.

She wakes for a while. Even in her darkest moment she has a smile. I am trying to make her comfortable but I only succeed in making her look like the Flying Nun.

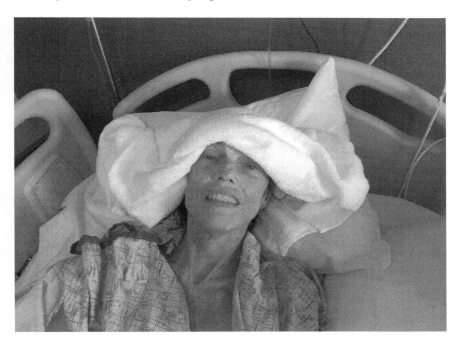

August 16

The vigil gets harder, the deterioration greater. Becky is on oxygen now. She can't use a straw anymore and I give her water and tea through a syringe. The nurse uses a small sponge on a stick to wet her mouth. Then she puts her medicine in apple sauce and feeds it to her. Taking her to the bathroom has become twice as hard. She loses her balance easily and her steps are small and uncertain. She must have had another seizure or a stroke. It's hard to tell because she twitches all the time.

I check messages on my phone. Many of them are words of encouragement for me. There is as much concern for the living as for the dying. Many offer prayers. I wonder what they are praying for because if it is for more life then they don't know Becky. This is not the quality of life she wished for. Here at the end I understand that. It was as if she had a finite amount of energy and she spent it ziplining, snorkeling, dancing, and just enjoying the beach. She did not spend it fighting cancer. She accepted that, and I realize as a nurse with a lifetime of experience she knew where that path led. Chemotherapy was not the answer for her.

I have my own prayers, I say them daily. I pray for her comfort and for no more pain. I pray for sweet Jesus to take her home with Him. I pray that she find her deceased loved ones there, just as we found each other in this world. I pray that somewhere beyond this facade she is living, that she is happy. But in a brief moment when she is awake I see otherwise. I bend over to hear what she is saying and she kisses me. The corner of her eye is wet.

Doctor Chopra comes for a visit. He stresses comfort and even writes it on the whiteboard as the care plan.

Becky is a vegetable. I turn on *The Young and the Restless*, move my chair into position, drop the guard rail on her bed and pet her gently. She snores, deep in some realm all her own. I cannot reach her. She sleeps clear through the next soap, *The Bold and the Beautiful*, her other favorite.

Two o'clock. The nurse comes in to check on her. She leans over her and asks in a loud voice, "How are you today?"
Becky opens her eyes and answers, clear and resonate. "I feel fine

164

today."

I am shocked. "She's been asleep all morning."

The nurse dispenses medicine and leaves. Minutes later Becky goes back to slurred speech. She has that lost look, and suddenly she can't communicate anymore. Just like Gina Rowlands in *The Notebook*.

But I am wrong. It's not a Gina Rowlands moment. Gradually over the next few hours she comes back to me, lucid and clear. I put her on the phone with Cherrie, then her mother. Dinner arrives, a pork chop with rice, gravy, and green beans. She eats voraciously, half a pork chop and a considerable amount of the sides. She has the strength to go to the bathroom and her steps are strong and sure.

Tracy, the hospice chaplain, comes by for a visit. He explains that David, the chaplain who came to visit us at home, is just that: a home visit chaplain. Tracy is the residential chaplain who has an office in this facility. He has read David's notes about us and he discusses a variety of things with Becky and I. When he's finished he asks, "Is there anything else I can do?"

"One more thing," I say. "David was going to officiate a ceremony for us. We wanted to do something like the reverse of marriage. A long time ago we made a vow. *'Till death us do part*. It's time to fulfill that vow."

I read the rough draft of the ceremony.[20] This is Becky's idea of a final ceremony, like undoing a marriage, but unlike a divorce, this separation is forced and final. My friend Mark told me about his wife dying, about the emptiness that follows. I remember how he looked off in the distance when he said, "There's no other feeling like waking up the next morning and knowing you'll never see her again. The empty bed, the empty heart. Nothing can describe that emotion or prepare you for it."

---

20 A transcript of the ceremony can be found in the Appendix of this book.

I think, *Maybe this ceremony will help.*

When it comes to reading her part of the ceremony there is a big "TBD", short for "To Be Determined". She hasn't provided any input yet and I promise the chaplain that I will finish this and send him a rough draft.

Tracy leaves. We have not set a date for the blessed event. Becky wanted to do this on the beach or in some natural surrounding, a park or picnic ground. This hospice would be a nice setting, out by the lake that her room overlooks. I brought the outfit she recently purchased and it's in the drawer along with her bling. Her health has been up and down so much lately I wonder if she will be able to say her vows.

I try to get her to tell me what she wants to say. I don't know what goes in place of TBD. Instead of filling in the blank, she announces that she is hungry. I feed her some soup but it does not satisfy her. "Get some Krystals." She says it clear and concise.

This statement tells me that she is getting better. It sounds so normal. As always, if she thinks she can eat it, I will go get it. "If I had my dive watch I'd take you with me."

She smiles. Laughter looks good on her.

My response needs some explanation. Let me tell you a Becky story.

When Becky was pregnant with Nick her water broke early in the pregnancy. She was admitted into University Hospital where the doctors put her on an inclined bed, her feet slightly elevated. This way, the water would build up in her uterus and not leak, giving Nick the best chance possible. They told her she needed to do this for six weeks minimum, possibly longer, maybe even until the birth.

She had a pregnancy appetite, craving chicken wings. At the end of the day I would leave the office, stop by the Hooters at the Jacksonville Landing, and then visit her at he hospital with a fresh batch of wings.[21]

After dinner I would put her in a wheelchair and take her downstairs to the lobby where there was a cafeteria with some video games. They were flat table, sit down machines, comfortable enough for her to enjoy without standing. We used to play a game where aliens would steal astronauts. She liked the way they would cry out "Help me, help me!" as the alien ships swooped down and kidnapped them. We also played a lot of Ms. PacMan, always getting excited when we reached the intermission after winning round two. The Pacs would meet and kiss, and we would often mimic them.

I used to wear a large dive watch. One day, just for fun, I took the watch and put it on Becky, covering her hospital bracelet so no one could see it. I pushed the wheelchair out the front door and into a nearby McDonald's where she got to order her own meal and eat something beside chicken wings and hospital food. We were so successful at his scam that we did it again. This time I took her home to the houseboat where she laid in her own bed and relaxed for a while. The boat was a peaceful place. We were on the Trout river across from the Jacksonville Zoo. The lapping water and the sounds of the animals calmed her. We spoke often of our future in this environment, as all couples do when a baby is on the way. I took the opportunity to speak to Bunner, leaning over the belly and saying, "You don't have to listen to those doctors. You're in Momma's womb. This is magic time, DNA time. You can fix this, everything they're worried about."

This was quite the opposite of the prayers I uttered when I was alone. "God, no matter what you give us, no matter what state he is born in, I will love him, even if it is only for three weeks on a respirator. Thy will be done, O Lord."

It's an easy promise to keep. I still love him. He's a great kid, or so

---

21 She still hates hospital food, as evidenced by her request for Krystals.

everyone says.

University Hospital was the last time we did the dive watch trick. I took her back there after the boat and we were quizzed on our whereabouts. "We looked for you everywhere. You weren't in the cafeteria. We had you paged." My paranoia made me think they had videos of me loading the hospital wheelchair in the back of the car and driving off with her.

The dive watch scam obviously would not work in the hospice, and things have changed in the last twenty five years, especially concerning hospitals and hospital security.

I go out for Krystals and when I get back, the car dies. Our car dies at a hospice! I laugh at the irony of it. Jimmy Buffet comes to mind. *If we couldn't laugh we would all go insane.* I call Teresa. She comes to pick me up, takes me home to her house.

She tells me a story about Steven when he was on his deathbed. "I didn't expect it," she says. "It just happened, very sudden. I always thought he would recover and get up,"

"I expect that too," I say. "Mary Jane told me she made a room ready for us at her house. I expect Becky will come home, get in the car, and we'll ride off into the sunset."

I am not being facetious, I actually believe this. The bucket tour will go on. I have Becky on my side. In her dementia, she thinks she is in a hospital and that she will be going home soon. I believe that is why she told the nurse in a clear voice that she is feeling fine. As a nurse Becky knows how to say the right thing and pass the test.

My sleep is restless that night. I wake up several times, finally at five AM, unable to go back to sleep.

August 17

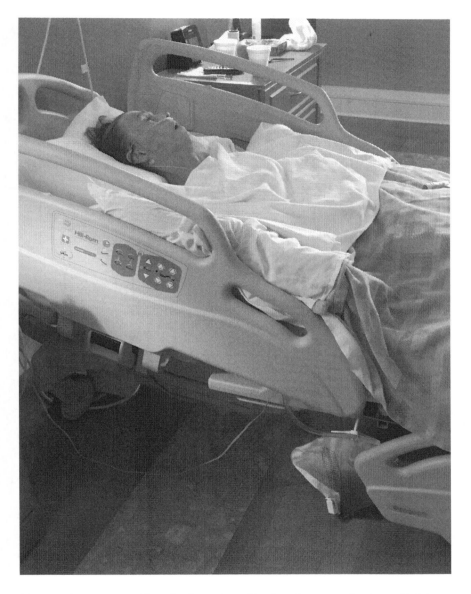

Teresa drops me off at the hospice. Becky does not look well this morning. Her color is good but she has a catheter now. She is still on oxygen. A nurse comes in and installs a subcutaneous port so they can give her morning medicine. She can't swallow anymore. She snores and they put atropine in her throat for comfort. She sleeps soundly. I sit in the window seat and watch her bag fill with urine. It is a lot more fluid than I have seen her drink in the last twenty four hours.

She snores. Don't tell her this but she snores. She will deny it and it will only make her angry, so don't tell her she snores. Nick and I have videos dating as far back as 1998 proving otherwise.

I pet her, try to wake her. I want to feed her the wonderful breakfast Community Hospice has made for her. Eggs and potatoes, grits, bacon.

She is unresponsive.

After it gets cold I eat the breakfast, saving enough to give Becky some if she happens to wake up.

Bridesmaid shows up. She tries to roust Becky but she is immobile. "Bridesmaid! Bridesmaid! It's me! Wake up," She and I both shake her. No response. It's already well past story time. She should be awake by now, up and discussing *The Young and the Restless*. Sharon immediately takes the role of nurse advocate, making sure the staff gives her something for her throat. She makes her comfortable, checks her for bed sores. She inspects the wound on her head.

A group of Community Hospice personnel enter the room. The Doctor is in charge and does all the talking, introducing the support staff, many of whom I have already met. These folks are professional, they know this business. They are doing the job she has done with the same dedication that she demanded of herself.

They leave and Sharon and I talk for a while. We try to roust her, talk some more. Sharon plays selections from the *Rocky Horror Picture Show*, reminding her of fun they had in the past. No effect. Sharon finally leaves.

My friends have come to my side in the hour of need. Jim Roe and Baby are on their way to tow my car to Mark who is going to fix it. Mark showed up this morning on his motorcycle, diagnosed the problem, and knows how to fix it. Broken timing belt. All the arrangements have been made and my focus remains Becky.

More friends arrive. Jeanie Weanie and Steve Berry, my old boss from the Jacksonville Marine Institute. A little while later, Jim Roe and Baby arrive. Becky wakes up and smiles when she sees them. A brief visit and they go right to work dealing with my car.

Becky can barely eat. I try to cut small pieces of chicken and feed it to her. She still has trouble with the soda straw. All she can eat is the cream of broccoli soup and the pudding. Doctors switch her to the comfort diet, smaller portions, easier to swallow. As I feed her she smiles. She has communication issues, all part of the problem she is having with her mouth. Again, when I bend my head close to her lips to hear what she is trying to say, she kisses me and smiles.

Between all these visitors, Becky is exhausted and soon she in a deep sleep. Her eyes twitch and she is smiling. I go home smiling too.

August 18

Sheree Hullander gives me a ride to the Hospice.

Becky sleeps. The fluid in her catheter bag is greater than what I remember her taking in yesterday. The color is dark amber. A nurse and an aide come in and turn her, bolstering her neck with rolled towels and extra pillows. She is comfortable, not snoring loudly like yesterday. There is a sense of peace in the room. The cable television is tuned to easy listening. She sleeps soundly. I eat her cold breakfast.
Friends call, relatives, loved ones. I give them updates. I try to awaken her several times. No response.

Sheree leaves. New visitors arrive, Lex and Jeanie Weanie. We huddle in the corner and talk. They let me know they are here for my support too. The outpouring of friends is overwhelming.

Alex entertains us with an interesting story. "Did I ever tell you about my near death experience?" he asks.

"I don't think so," I say.

"It was back in college when I was learning to dive," he begins. "I was just getting certified. A friend was forming a dive club. They planned a dive at a rock quarry near Cape Girardeau, Missouri. They told me that if I went along, the instructor would certify me. I went along, suited up, and jumped in the quarry before my dive buddy. I knew he was right behind me so I started my descent. I had a flashlight. Visibility was low and it got darker the deeper you went. I was down about ninety feet and it was pretty dark. I turned my flashlight off to see what it was like. Pitch black! Awesomely creepy.

"I pushed the button on my flashlight to turn it back on. It didn't work. At the depth I was at, the button never popped back out to reset the switch. I started to ascend, thinking I could go up far enough to ease the pressure and pop the switch.

"I hit solid rock above my head. I had somehow stumbled into a cave and was trapped, pitch black, with no indication where the entrance was. A funny feeling came over me.

"Suddenly I was outside my body, positioned about ten feet away, looking back at myself. The cavern was bright and lit up. I looked at myself and said, *What are you going to do now?*

Behind the lit walls of the cave I felt the presence of people, beings looking at me through a thin veil. They called to me. Suddenly I was back in my body. There was a tunnel of white light up ahead and I was moving towards it on a conveyor belt. I got closer to the end. I felt a presence, a large masculine being. He stood behind all these people that were watching and encouraging me as I rode down the tunnel. In a clear voice, he said, *Uh uh. No. Not time yet.*

"I was split again, a replay of my original predicament, backed out of the tunnel and outside my body looking at myself. I said again, *Well, what are you going to do now?*

I was in my body then. I put my hands on the roof of the cave to orient myself. I figured if I moved in a line, the cave had to get smaller as I went deeper. Feeling for the bottom with my flipper I tried to make my way along. I saw a dim light in the distance and I headed toward it. Turned out to be my dive buddy shining his light around looking for me. I shot right past him, gave him the hand signal that I was done and heading for the surface."

"That's quite a story," I say.

"I haven't told it to many people," he says.

"What do you make of it?" I ask.

"That there is an afterlife," he says. "And it was not my time."

Becky wakes up and I spend time trying to feed her. She eats some pudding and drinks a tiny amount of tea. I keep a towel handy and use a napkin to wipe her chin. She is losing control of her mouth. Alex and Jean retreat, leaving me alone with her for some quality time.

Slowly she falls back asleep. After a while Sheree shows up with Diana and her dog Kimora. Becky is not even aware that they are here. She continues to sleep soundly. Diana and Sheree leave, but not before Sheree gives me the keys to her car to use.

"You may need these," she says.

I am grateful, thinking that I may need it in the middle of the night.

I sit there on the window seat working on this book. I am thinking that I have only my own Becky story to add, I've set enough of other people's down. It has come to this. The Bucket Tour will end here. There will be no more visits, no more travel, only one last trip to take. One I cannot take her on. I am no longer the driver on this tour. And so, here goes.

When Becky was young and living with me, in a time before her first bout with cancer, she was attending classes at Florida Junior College in Jacksonville (now Florida Community College at Jacksonville). It came time for her class project, I remember her telling me about it after class. It was about geriatric nursing. She went into class with a bunch of supplies. Eye patches, gauze bandages, dive weights, lots of surgical tape. When it was time for her presentation she prepared every student differently. Some wore eye patches. Some had fingers taped together, wore leg splints, or had dive weights attached to their arm. Some wore earplugs, others were blinded completely. One had their right arm bound at their side.

She gave some of them a card, individualized instructions for them to follow. Instructions like: "Every five minutes, say something crazy", "Point to imaginary people and call them out by name", and "Yell for a nurse every now and then", and even "You can't talk at all, just moan."

She lectured about geriatrics, about what it would be like for these young men and women, college classmates, to grow up and face old age. She talked passionately about care for the aged. Listed common diseases and their symptoms. She predicted the need for caregivers and support. Then, in their bound state, she made them all play bingo.

She got an A plus on the project.

Becky knew what to expect. When we lived in Kodiak she was the charge nurse of the geriatric wing. She told me stories about the patients. One day I was visiting her and a patient asked me, "Did you get that Caribou for the Mayor?"

"What caribou?" I asked.

He pointed down the hall. "It's over there on that sled." Then he pointed at Becky. "Check with that moose girl."

She helped a lot of people find their way in the dark. More than once she had me stop the car at the scene of an accident. We once stopped at a bad wreck on the corner of Atlantic Boulevard and San Pablo Road. She performed CPR on one of the victims, passing the care to the EMTs when they arrived.

Countless friends and relatives have called her for advice when they were hurt or ailing. She was everybody's Mama. She was always bedside at the hospital when her loved ones needed a caregiver or a nurse advocate.

That is the sum of her life. She cares. She cares about her children, her patients, her loved ones, even small dogs and animals. She makes us all laugh. She loves us for who we are.

Everyone she touches learns something from her. At a recent trip to a Waffle House she spoke passionately with a young waitress, encouraged to follow her dream of being a nurse. Becky never forgets where she comes from, and she never will.

I talk to people we may never see, people who are scheduled for stops on the bucket tour when we head back to Seattle. My sister, Louise, Tommy Tuscon, Craig and Joan, Allen Dillon, Tara. There are countless stories of her floating out there, things these people and others have reminded me about. Things she has done and accomplished. I wrote a few of them down in the appendix.

I don't know if I have the time to document them all. This is my best attempt, and I would rather spend the time caring for her than writing about her.

It has been a long day and I feel it. Despair sets in. I pack up my computer and go to Teresa's for some much needed rest.

August 19

Becky has changed overnight. Her color does not look good. Her breathing is short and raspy, not deep and peaceful. It's as if she is struggling to catch her breath. She used to tell me that most of her hospice patients died of kidney failure or lung failure. She is running a fever, a little over a hundred. The urine output bag is dark and cloudy.

It's her show now. Observations of the symptoms may lead to a diagnosis. Pneumonia is suspected, but they don't do tests in hospice. Best we can do is make her comfortable. The prediction is it could happen anytime, maybe even in the next forty eight hours.

I talk to her. Her eyes roll and her brow furrows and twitches. I don't know if she can hear me or if it autonomic motions because of the drugs. He eyes are not quite shut, but this could be an indicator that she is close.

I hold her hand and talk to her. I tell her it's okay to go. Her eyes roll and she looks like she's trying to say something. Hearing is the last thing to go, didn't someone tell me that the other day? I want her to hear me and I tell her that I love her. The next words come automatically, they have run through my mind hundreds of times in the last few weeks. Gently, I lean over her and say, "I love you. I forgive you. Please forgive me."

Her breath is quick and shallow. Her eyes move, the lids still open in narrow slits. My inside voice gives me strength to continue.

It's okay. It's okay to say it. You're going to have to say it sooner or later.

I gather myself, my voice cracking like an adolescent choir boy. "Goodbye."

"It's okay to go, my love." I'm talking away now, petting her gently. She has a gurgling sound, fluid aspirating in her lungs. Her head hangs to the side, her mouth open, her eyes moving behind the half open slits. Her eyebrows move, facial expressions that say something to my heart.

I brace myself for the day, huddling on the window seat that overlooks the lake. I don't feel up to the task today. I feel weak and hungry. The hospice cafe is closed so I tell the nurse I'm going to grab something to eat and I'll be right back.

Mark calls about my car. I need to run some money out to him for parts. I silently thank Sheree for letting me borrow her car. On the way back I stop at Waffle House. I need comfort food. My spirit is heavy and sallow, empty and in need of nourishment.

I get back to the hospice at the same time as Audra, Bridesmaid's daughter. I set up my computer and prepare for the vigil. We talk to her, imagining that the contortions in her face, the tremors in her lips, are her way of answering us. Audra is saying a Rosary, a Catholic ritual that is like a power prayer. I am pacing like a cat and I walk down the hall to use the bathroom. As I'm coming back, Audra flags me from the room and I quicken my pace.

"There's a change in her respiration," she says.

I look down at her. She is breathing like she is trying to catch her breath. I hold her hand and tell her it's okay. I pet her and talk to her. It is sudden, her last breaths slow. Eternity passes as I wait for the next one. They are long deep breaths, sighs. Sighs of relief, not of regret.

177

The pain is over. As easy as that her eyes close. I think she is asleep. I hold her hand. It is Audra who gets the nurse. I'm still not processing it. Even as the nurse puts a stethoscope to her chest I look down expecting one more breath.

It's not so. The nurse is talking about what happens now. We can have this room as long as it takes. "Are there family members on their way?"

"No," I say.

The nurse leaves. Audra stays with me a while, then says, "I'll let you have some time alone."

"I need it," I say. "Thank you for saying the Rosary."

"I asked God to relieve her suffering. As soon as I finished the five decades, that's when those last few breaths came. Thank you for allowing me to be here with her and you." She leaves.

I text messages, make some calls, grieve. Cry like a wounded child in the window seat. I pack up my computer. In the drawer I retrieve her white dress and flowing top. The bling and the new shoes she bought for the ceremony that we planned. I look at her and I know she is at peace.

"I love you. Goodbye."

I make a note of it. She died at 11:15 in the morning, August 19. It has been exactly four months to the day since the doctor told her she had four months to live. I'm glad she spent it wisely, living the kind of life she loved.

I walk outside, into the light. The sun is shining, it's a hot Florida day. Audra is beside me. My friends Lex and Jeanie Weanie are waiting on a bench by the parking lot. They greet me with love and compassion. I know I will be okay.

178

Ending

I have this thought, kind of a waking dream, nothing to do with reality.

I am driving down a street with Becky enjoying the scenery. She wants a chili dog and there is a drive-in restaurant up ahead. We pull in and place the order. The server that brings our food is a beautiful young girl on roller skates, a smile as bright and as wide as any. When we finish eating, she comes back to get the empty tray. As she picks it up, it disappears and she turns into an angel.

Becky smiles and the angel skates over to my side of the car and opens the door. "I'll take it from here," she whispers.

I slowly get out of the car and she takes my place. I lean against the window and look over at Becky and say, "I guess I'll catch up with you later."

The angel smiles and puts the car in reverse. "It's okay," she says. "Enjoy yourself. We'll see you at the resort tonight."

My heart feels light, purified and peaceful. The car reverses and turns, carefully pulling out into the busy street.

THE END

APPENDIX

Becky Can Cook

Anyone who knew Becky knew she could cook. Jay told me that the oven was broken one Thanksgiving and she cooked the entire Thanksgiving dinner on the stove top, including turkey, bread, stuffing, and yams. I got that beat. Thanksgiving following the hurricane in St. Thomas, she cooked it on a Coleman stove. Heck, she cooked all our meals on a Coleman stove until the power came back on. I was impressed with the sheer variety of things she could cook on it. In Alaska I once watched her make biscuits on a camp fire. She made a funny looking tent out of aluminum foil and put it on a metal plate to cook them. That's not all she could do on a campfire. I've eaten fried pies made out of foraged salmon berries. She was dubbed the fire goddess by appreciative Spit Rats in Homer one summer.

At one point in life she acquired quality cookware. She sold

Pampered Chef just to get the demonstration kit. Using these tools she catered many events including Jack and Sara's wedding, the annual NickFest which ran for three or four years, and untold birthdays and parties. She was always a major contributor to food events in the workplace.

At Thanksgiving she would invite any FEMA people on deployment, or people who had nowhere else to go, usually twenty or more would show up. We used to go around the room and have everyone say something they were thankful for. I was always thankful for Becky's good cooking,

One of Becky's typical Christmas spreads.

According to her mother this desire for cooking began early in her life. She got an Easy Bake Oven for Christmas one year and fell in love with it. Her parents enjoyed watching her mix pre-weighed packets of powder with liquid, pouring it in a pan, and heating it under a light bulb. It wasn't as good as her later cooking, but it was

183

a start. Becky would pop out a sheet of cookies and proudly walk towards her parents with it. Mary Jane can still remember turning to her husband and saying, "Okay, Jimmy, it's your turn to eat the cookie."

One of her most remarkable cooking accomplishments was catering her mother's wedding to Daddy Frank. Everything was set for the big date. Four days before the wedding the venue for the reception burned down. Frank should have taken this as an omen, but they decided to proceed with the wedding anyway. We had just built a large deck at our house with a view of the Blue Ridge Mountains. With a fully equipped kitchen (thanks to Pampered Chef and KitchenAid) it was a good substitute location. The cake was already ordered. At least that problem was solved.

Becky planned a menu of two options, lasagna or chicken. She and Mary Jane went to Sam's club and bought the ingredients and set to work on the prep. Our neighbor Patrice borrowed a hundred chairs and a dozen tables from the Synagogue for us. Becky hired two young girls to serve the food, classmates of Nick's that we went to church with. The logistics were incredible. I was part of the "Git gone team". We got to see the wedding but it was our job to leave immediately after the ceremony and head to the house to get things set up for the reception. Eighty seven people showed up, at least that was the final plate count. Needless to say, the event was a success.

Nick worked side by side with his mother over the last few years. Always her caregiver, ever her son, he prepared countless dishes for her and with her. Over the course of writing this book, we have captured not only her stories, but also some of her best recipes.

BACON HONEY DRESSING

Matt always wanted to bottle and sell this one, but it's best fresh. Honestly, have you ever seen solidified bacon fat in the fridge?

Ingredients: 4 pieces of bacon
1 cup mayonnaise
1-2 oz honey

Cook the bacon and save the bacon grease. Mix the grease with 1 cup mayonnaise, add 1-2 ounces of honey to sweeten the taste to your liking. Crumble bacon, mix, and top your favorite salad.

SOUTHWEST CARIBBEAN DRESSING

½ Cup olive oil[22]
juice of 1 lime
¼ cup sugar
2 tsp. Cumin
2 cloves garlic
salt, fresh ground pepper to taste

ITALIAN DRESSING

Olive oli
Balsamic Vinegar
sugar
Italian seasoning
garlic
onion powder
salt and pepper

---

22 For less fat omit olive oil.

BLUE CHEESE DRESSING

1 cup mayonnaise
1 cup sour cream
½ cup whipping cream (or half and half)
2 cloves garlic, pressed
½ tsp. Worchestershire Sauce
½ tsp. Onion powder
½ tsp, salt
½ tsp. Freshly ground black pepper
4-8 ounces crumbled blue cheese or Gorgonzola
for spicy dressing, add ½ tsp. Tobasco

Gently mix together all ingredients . Allow to sit, refrigerated, for at least 2 hours so that the flavors have time to blend.

CAESAR DRESSING

½ cup olive oil
1 clove garlic
½ lemon
1 tsp. Worstershire
1 tsp. Anchovy paste
2 tablespoons mayonnaise
Parmesan cheese

CORN DIP

1 can creamed corn
1 can Mexicorn
1 can green chilis
1 cream cheese
Mix in crock pot

FRIED RICE

In 2 tablespoons butter, chop finely and fry: garlic, green pepper, mushrooms, onion, carrot. Add cooked rice. Stir. Add 2 tablespoons soy sauce and stir. Add 1 egg, beaten.

MEATBALLS

¼ cup onion
green pepper
2 – 3 garlic cloves

Saute onion, pepper, garlic in olive oil

1 lb. Ground beef
1 lb ground pork (or sausage)
½ cup bread crumbs
1 tsp. Oregano, 1 tsp. Basil (or 2 tsp. Italian seasoning)
1 egg

Mix together. Form into small balls. Fry or bake, then drain on paper towels.

EGGPLANT PARMESAN

Start by preparing spaghetti sauce: Combine, fry and drain 2-3 links hot Italian sausage, 1 onion, and three cloves garlic. Add 1 Prego and 1 can diced tomatoes Italian style (S&W brand). Add 1 cup wine and ¾ cup half and half.

Slice eggplant, let weep. (♪ While my eggplant gently weeps... ♫) prepare batter: 1 cup cornmeal, ½ cup pancake mix, 1 tsp. Garlic salt, ½ tsp. onion powder, 1 tsp. Oregano. Roll. Set in fridge while you wind down. Get up and roll in egg mixture (2 eggs, beat with splash of cream.), then in flour. Fry until brown.

Line casserole dish with eggplant. Sprinkle with Parmesan cheese and mozzarella. Cover with fresh spinach (torn), mushrooms, and sauce. Cook at 350 degrees for 45 minutes. Remove, top with mozzarella cheese.

ALFREDO SAUCE

Finely dice 2 tblsp. Onion and 2 garlic cloves and fry until transparent in butter. Drain on a paper towel. Combine:

2 Cups half and half
1 cup heavy cream
2 tablespoons flour
¼ cup Parmesean cheese
salt and pepper to taste.

Add garlic and onion. Heat until thickened.

NICK'S FAVORITE

This one is so named because, well it's Nick and mine favorite.
Becky cooked it a lot for us. It's one of the first dishes Nick learned
before he went off to college.

Ingredients: .

  1 1/2 pounds cubed round steak, cut into thin strips or ground
  beef

  1 packet of French Onion soup mix

  All-purpose flour.

  2 tablespoons olive oil.

  2 tablespoons butter.

  1 medium onion, sliced.

  8 ounces fresh mushrooms, sliced.

  1 (10 3/4-ounce) can beef broth.

  Dollop of Sour cream topping

  Flat noodles, Mueller's preferred

Directions

Sprinkle the steak strips with French Onion Soup Mix to lightly
cover them, and then dust with flour. In a large skillet, quickly
brown them on both sides in the olive oil and butter. Remove the
steak from the pan. Add the onion slices and mushrooms to the pan
drippings. Saute for a few minutes, until the onion is tender.
Sprinkle with 1 teaspoon flour. Put the steak back into the pan with
the onion and mushrooms. Add the mushroom soup and beef broth.
Cook over low heat for about 30 minutes, covered. Adjust
seasoning to taste, adding salt and pepper, as needed. Stir in some
sour cream the last few minutes, right before you serve. Serve over
cooked noodles with a dollop of sour cream on top.

SURFER SPECIAL (modified from Ellen's Kitchen)

1 - medium to large potato

1 slice American cheese

2 – strips bacon, cooked

2 – eggs, fried over easy

butter

¼ cup chopped onions (optional)

1 – slice wheat toast

Grate the potato and fry in oil to create hash browns. Add onions if desired. Place on plate and add a little butter and the slice of cheese. Put bacon on top and then the eggs. Serve with slice of toast.

PIMENTO CHEESE

5 - 8 oz. Cheeses. One or two should be Monterrey Jack, the others Cheddar (pick what you like, sharp, mild, or medium, or mix them up)

1 – 8 oz. block cream cheese (Becky always uses Philadelphia Cream Cheese. Use good ingredients to achieve good results.)

1 to 1 ½ cups of mayonnaise

1 – 7 oz. jar of pimentos

1 – teaspoon sugar

Grate the cheese into two different sizes for texture. Add the mayonnaise, cream cheese, and pimentos and stir. Add sugar and stir to finish. Best served in the Southern tradition by slathering on over-processed white bread buttered in mayonnaise.

PASTA SALAD

This one was from an entry in the Evergreen Hospital Recipe Contest in 2009. Don't know if it won or not.

1 lb. Pasta shells
Juice of ½ lime
¼ tsp. Grated lime peel
1 clove pressed garlic
¼ cup Pepe Lopez crème of coconut
½ cup half and half or heavy whipping cream (cream tastes better)
¼ cup mayonaise
¼ cup chopped onion
¼ cup chopped red pepper
1 small can pineapple chunks – well drained
finely chopped hot pepper to taste, app. ¼ tsp
2 heirloom red tomatoes cut into bite sized pieces
1 cup coconut

Boil pasta and drain. Preheat oven to 350. Turn off oven and put in coconut spread out on baking sheet. Check and stir every 5 minutes or so until browned and crunchy.

Toss together all ingredients except for coconut. Chill 1-2 hours then top with coconut and serve.

TURDS

This delectable treat is so named because it looks just like it says. These are hand rolled peanut butter toilet loafs dipped in chocolate. Once they are made and laid out to eat, they don't stay around for long. Becky's mom, Mary Jane, is credited with laying the first turds. Wait. That didn't sound right. Let's say she originated this recipe. Becky improved it. She used to make them every year for Christmas. She stored them in holiday tins to keep them fresh.

Nick made turds for Becky's memorial in Seattle. I learned from watching him that he cooks like his mother. By that I mean, ingredients aren't quite exact, there is leeway to experiment, and no matter how much you deviate from the recipe, turds always turn out great. This recipe is tried and tested.

1+ cups confection sugar

4 packages graham crackers

6-8 tablespoons butter

10-20+ oz. Walnuts

full 1lb jar (16oz) crunchy peanut butter

dash of vanilla extract

salt to taste (if needed)

Semi-sweet Chocolate (chips or blocks, either will do.)

Crush the graham crackers until they are powdery. No need to pulverize them, just make sure they are in small pieces. Add the confection sugar and the walnuts. Add more walnuts if you kike a nutty taste. Mix well. On the stove melt butter and peanut butter stirring continuously. Add a dash of vanilla extract to that. While warm combine it all and mix well. You can add salt but usually peanut butter has a good amount in it.

Once the mixture is consistent, press into turd like shapes in the palm of your hand. Set on parchment paper and let harden over an hour.

Melt chocolate over double boiler. Becky used a microwave, but it's easy to burn if you're not careful. Dip turds in melted chocolate. Nick says it's a good balance to only dip the top half of the turd in chocolate, but in my opinion they don't quite get that turd look unless fully dipped.

Mmmmmm,,,, Lovely!

COFFEE ENEMA

This recipe was found in Becky's effects, scribbled on a postcard from Mr. Steve Harmon.

1 ½ quarts distilled water

3 tablespoons dry coffee

Combine ingredients. Boil for 3 minutes, then simmer for 20 minutes. Cool and strain. You know the rest.

FAVORITE MOVIES

An Affair to Remember
Armageddon
Beauty and the Beast (Disney versions)
The Birdcage
Bronco Billy
Casablanca
Choose Me
Cinderella (Rogers and Hammerstein and animated versions)
Desperately Seeking Susan
Die Hard
Doctor Zhivago
Ever After
Legally Blonde
Living Out Loud
Outrageous
Overboard
Paint Your Wagon
Pretty Woman
South Pacific
Sweet Home Alabama
The Parent Trap
Thelma and Louise
While She Was Out

FAVORITE SAYINGS

"Wish with one hand and shit in the other and see which comes true first." Becky's mama, Mary Jane Bland Fortner, has to get partial credit for this one, but Becky repeated it often. It's an old Southern phrase.

"Bless your heart." Like the previous quote, this is also an old Southern phrase. Like most of these phrases, they come with a twist. This phrase was probably born out of the code of the South which says "If you can't say something nice, don't say anything at all." Nearest I can figure this is a way for those who can't keep their mouth shut to let someone know in a very polite way that they are an idiot, but what do I know, as I keep saying, I'm just that Yankee boy that married Becky Jane.

"You're wearing *that*?" A nice way of of informing someone that they may not be properly dressed for the occasion.

"Are you awake?" This phrase must be repeated in a gravelly voice, enough to wake someone from a deep sleep. It replaced an earlier phrase that went: "I'm here. I'm bored. Wake up and play with me."

"Hurry up. Mamma ain't waiting on you all day." Used to gently nudge anyone who might be dawdling and holding up the group.

"Yeah, but it's all garage." Research indicates this may have originated with Mary Jane. Used in response to: "That's a really big house." One time on vacation we saw a condominium under construction. I said to Becky, "Those look like some nice condos." She looked over at them and said, "Yeah, but it's all garage." Sure enough, she was right. It was mostly a huge parking garage.

"Acid is like a box of chocolates, You never know what you're gonna get."

"Close that door! You're letting all that bought air out." Bought air referring to any of that expensive air that is heated or air conditioned.

"Act like you got good sense." A common Southern saying, repeated endlessly by Southern moms everywhere, and Becky is no exception.

"If you got a bunch of young'ins, that's all you got is a bunch of young'ins." Said after observing kids bouncing on your couch, breaking dinnerware, or otherwise destroying any household item you ever owned or cherished.

FAVORITE SONGS

Nick and Chris compiled a huge playlist on YouTube for the
Seattle Memorial and were spot on. This list is in no way complete.
Becky wrote this down in a notebook while she was still alive.

Freebird – Skynard[23]
I Can't Help Falling In Love With You – King Elvis
Hello Dolly – by Barbara
Angie – Stones
Oh Darling – Beatles
Rain on the Roof – Lovin' Spoonful
Did You Ever Have to Make Up Your Mind
Out My Back Door – Credence Clearwater
Downtown – Petula Clark
Love Me Tender – Elvis
Reason to Believe – Rod Stewart
Someone Saved My Life Tonight – Elton John
I'm Not in Love – 10 cc's
New York New York – Sinatra
I Will Survive – Gloria Gaynor
Antonio's Song – Michael Franks

---

23 Joan works at a radio station: 91.9 FM, available on the web
worldwide at krvm.org. As a memorial to Becky the station will
play Freebird every November 15, her birthday.

The Bereavement Ceremony

Note: This ceremony was never performed.

DAVID (or TRACY): Presenting for the last time, the bride and groom, Becky and Nick. In so much as having made a vow thirty eight years ago, until death do us part; now is the time to fulfill that obligation, the time to say goodbye.

NICK: Becky, love has been more than a sustaining force for the both of us. Truly, together we have exceeded the sum of our individual talents and abilities. I am already less of a man, and although hard it may be, I have things yet to accomplish, things I must do before my time comes to an end. They will be harder without you here, but you live on in my heart, and I need only go there to seek your help and guidance.

Forever may you live in the glory of God and life everlasting. Find your heavenly mansion, no more hovels, no more broken houses. Let love carry you away and pull you towards those that wait for you. Daddy. Steven. Kathy Carver. Rod and Mary. Dottie. Bill the bunny.

BECKY: TBD

DAVID (or TRACY) : In so much as Becky and Nick may see each other for the very last time on this Earth, I pronounce it okay to part, one to travel beyond this realm, one to stay home and pack up before leaving. It is the natural order of life and the time.

What is the primary cause of death?

Being born.

Becky, you have lived a good life. Some say that at the end we face Nothing. You have nothing to fear, nothing to regret, nothing but love.

God waits for you. It is all right to leave your husband and go to Him.

BECKY: TBD

NICK: (Reads Poem:)

The Goodbye

Remember my dear, remember my dear,
        We've both been here before
Remember my sweet, close to your death
        Beyond us lies so much more
The pain is over, the sadness ended
        The crippled body gone
A new one waits, God's next creation
        Life *does* go on and on
So rest my sweet, I'll hold your hand
        And send you on your way
I'll see you later, don't wait for me
        I'll come home at the end of my day

I love you, I forgive you, please forgive me, goodbye.
Goodbye.

BECKY: I have loved you, you have forgiven me, I forgive you.
Goodbye

DAVID (or TRACY): You may now kiss the bride.

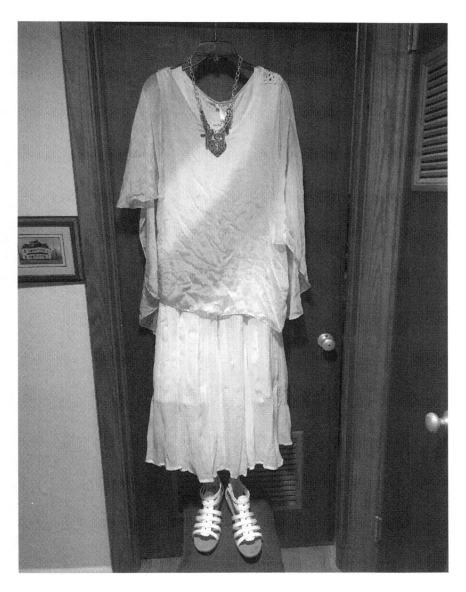

Becky's bereavement outfit that she planned to wear for the
ceremony. The tag is still on the dress. I don't have the heart to
return it.

Autumn wrote this:

When a person leaves us, we feel many emotions and go through a grieving process without realizing it. Each in our own and different way. However, we have one thing in common. We all are left behind with memories. Becky will remain with us all in our minds, our dreams, our hearts and our senses forever.

Maybe it's a song on the radio, a smell, or a familiar feeling of dejavu that brings her back to us - back so strongly that we stop because the force of her memory is so alive that it's as if she is with us in the present. In the moment again. And we will remember her. We will remember being with her during some amazingly fun times. We will remember her smile, her laughter, her delicious meals, her ability to listen to others, her beliefs that standing up for herself and for others is always the right thing to do.

She once told me a story about a patient of hers while she was a hospice nurse. The lady loved birds and took care of them and it was almost time for the lady to pass and she was keeping a close eye on her. When it was getting almost time, she looked out her window and there were birds everywhere. She said she couldn't count how many birds because there were so many. So, she just kept holding the ladies hand and after a little while; she passed. Then, all the birds left. Becky said it was one of the most amazing things she had seen as a hospice nurse. She said it changed how she saw death with her patients. It didn't always have to be a grueling sad story. Sometimes, it could be an amazing story.

Becky will live on in each of us. In her friends and family; In the stories we tell, in the recipes we cook, in the dreams we have, and in our hearts and feelings.

Jay's Rebuttal to the God Damn Tea Story

Jay said he couldn't remember the GD Tea Story. He did have something to say about it, though.

G.D. Tea My Rebuttal

I mostly worked. The only time I didn't work was the winter Nashville froze. I was planting trees and the ground was frozen.

Anyway if I was upset about ice-tea, it was probably after working an 18-hour day planting trees or laying sod (we were working downtown by street light sometimes).

If you have ever been so dirty you had to undress before you enter the house and go straight to the shower, if you know what it's like to be able to light a kitchen match off of the callouses on your hand, and don't drink beer, you know what it means to want to have some God Damn Tea when you get home.

- Jay Eklond, October 30, 2017

POEMS AND WRITINGS BY BECKY

BECKY'S ACCOUNT OF HURRICANE MARILYN

I've waited a month to write it all down. It's easier to write about it as you can see the light at the end of the tunnel.

Marilyn came into my life during a real bad time – the computer not working, Nick not working, the stairs breaking, the truck breaking, thieves stealing our possessions, that bitch stealing our passion. Broke, frustrated, hating my job, my life, etc. No bonus from HSSI. Walls where Nick used to be. Working, cleaning and doing laundry on days off. While Nick is out diving and partying all the time. Yep, Marilyn got there just in the Nick of time.

It was the usual day. Nick picked me up from work early. At least she wasn't leaning on the car looking all pussy eyed at him. We gave the two new nurses a ride home to Nick's disdain, but he lightened up as he realized they were in a real bind – not even enough money for a cab ride home. I heard they stayed after the storm – no money for air fare.

About 6PM we watched some big birds being sucked into Tunsey Bay. Five of them. One by one sinking one last time into the turbulent water.

We played some backgammon – about the only past time we shared anymore, and just meandered around without electricity.

At 9:30 Nicks were asleep. I couldn't sleep. No one expected much, but I was still anxious. I called my mother. She put the phone up to the TV on the Weather Channel and maps were saying it was just passing over St. Thomas and was not bad. They would begin the rebuilding at 7AM. I told my mother I loved her and it was something about hearing your mother's voice that helps you stay calm. The wind was beginning to pick up so we hung up and I

put away a few things in the kitchen and went to sleep – but I didn't sleep. It kept getting worse. Nick woke up and we just laid there until it got to the glass breaking stage so we ran into the closet (and Nick got two mattresses). Then we cuddled under them and $Nick_2$ fell asleep. We laid there with our feet out until it got to the ear splintering, yelling in your ear, freight train fast approaching stage. He held on tight to us both and we held on to each other and the mattress over us. We prayed for survival. We clung to each other, afraid to let go, afraid to move. Somehow during this time we became one again. Together in a weird combination of fear and strength, we became two parts of a whole, whose purpose was to be brave and strong for that little boy and for each other. He would wake up and whimper occasionally, grab tightly to us both and drift back off.

Time became frozen – a foreign concept. I couldn't tell how much time had passed. At one point I had to pee so bad I couldn't wait. I grabbed one of the Zook's[24] rugs and went for it. As I was doing this I stretched out my leg and moved the mattress. Above my head was sky. One of those trees uprooting must have been the roof. The wind was so loud and vicious that even the heavy plate glass doors breaking sounded like a fine crystal goblet tinkling as it hits the floor. Roofs and walls sounded like slats in the windows being blown out. When the eye passed Nick wanted to move us to the kitchen so he got up and went to scout out a route. I thought it was odd that he stood and peed in the hallway, but it didn't quite register that there was no other room out there. N_2 and I clung to each other while we waited forever for Nick. I was so afraid a gust would come up and hit him with debris or blow him away. Looking up at the sky during the lull was magnificent. Gray high clouds whipping by like in a scary movie. It was pure relief when Nick made it back for Part II.

The first half I had to pee so bad it gave me something to focus on. Once I peed I had nothing but raw nerve to stand on. I thought about comforting times like sitting on Maw Maw Bland's lap while she sang "Reuben Reuben" and "Jesus Loves the Little Children",

---

24 The Zooks ownwd the house we were renting

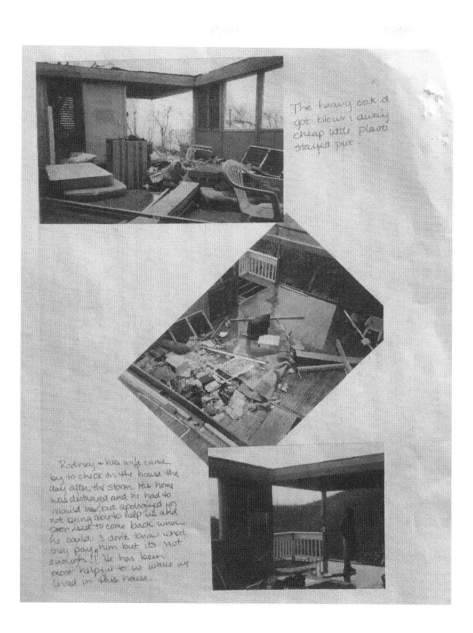

The heavy oak d
got blown away
cheap little plasti
stayed put.

Rodney + his wife came
by to check on the house the
day after the storm. His home
was distroyed and he had to
rebuild his, but apologized for
not being able to help us and
promised to come back when
he could. I don't know what
they pay him but its not
enough !! He has been
most helpful to us while we
lived in this house.

and being sick at home from school and my Daddy bringing me chicken noodle soup and Dr. Peppers, Nick while I was pregnant with N_2 and many loving and secure times, but mostly I would remember how I felt when he would pop his head in the door of my room with that big goofy smile and a treat, and kiss me and my belly. I felt like no matter what ever happened to me, we would face it together and Nick would protect me from hurt. I thought about his face while I was having the baby, the way he looked when he first saw his son. That was the way pure love looks.

There was no way for us to get to the kitchen. I don't know why we didn't go to the bathroom. Didn't think of it. So we held on for an even worse nightmare ride into hell and back. The floor was swaying beneath us, the wall behind us was heaving. I began to ask the Lord to please please let the sun come up. We prayed and I sang "You Are My Sunshine" to N_2. We were both clammy from the adrenaline rush. The mattress was getting heavy with water and smelling very very bad and it was not warm anymore. Everything was soaked and water was dripping everywhere. Just when I was ready to say OK I can't do this anymore it began to ease up. We could talk again. The sun was coming up. We went into the kitchen to try to get dryer but it was just as cold and drippy so we went to the bathroom. It was shocking to walk through empty space where walls had been, shattered glass everywhere, furniture gone or smashed up in a different corner of a different room. Nick got us food and water and stuffed Monopril and Xanax in my mouth. Soon we heard voices yelling outside, our neighbors Harry and Lori checking on us, amazed that we were still alive. N_2 and I fell asleep for a while, sheer exhaustion on my part. When we got up we began to really take in what had happened and to begin the long and painful and joyful survey of what was lost and what was spared. We did a lot of holding on to us all. We sort of moved in a pack, just walking from room to room looking and staring in disbelief. I tried to dry out clothes I found, but it kept gusting and raining. We laughed and shared a knowing look when we found the camcorder sitting perfectly on a shelf out of the case, but sitting there like someone carefully placed it there. And the scuba gear on the floor not damaged, not even moved from the exact spot it was

209

left in. Barney! The baby clothes panels. After a while we went out to see the neighbors and we made plans to cook our salmon and filet mignon and Lori had shrimp. We could all sleep at Bruce's cottage that was not damaged. Lori's house was flattened. So was Harry's. We grilled our dinner and went to sleep when it got dark on mattresses with the plastic still on them. What was the rest of the island like? We heard Jo Ann the psychotic psychiatric nurse screaming, watched her walk around like a zombie saying inappropriate things like, "I'm glad I moved. This could have been me. I just can't deal with this, etc." We saw and heard no one else that day. Just gusts of wind and bursts of rain all day. No connection with the rest of the island or the world. No helicopters. No birds. No insects. No traffic. Everything was dead but us. It was strange and apocalyptic. Your conscious mind is in shock, nerves frayed, tired, trembly all over, heart racing shaky, wondering if its really over. There must be a safety valve in the brain that cuts off any thoughts beyond now. You go into a post devastation period where you have to do something even if it's wrong. Like hanging clothes walking over shattered glass in wet shoes and no socks, urine soaked wet clothes. One of the first conscious things we did was change clothes. Of course these got wet soon enough. We were able to take showers that day because the cistern was higher than the house and worked on gravity feed. We filled buckets. This was our shower for the next week. Buckets of cold water.

Day two Sunday. We got up, waking up hoping this was a bad nightmare. It wasn't. It is all death and devastation all around. The same deafening quietness. No movement anywhere. We sat on the Zook's stairs and ate the last of our cereal and milk. Disbelief is still the line of thinking. We decide to try to get out to a phone to call our folks. Out on the main road it became sickeningly clear that we were not an isolated tornado. The entire Anna's Retreat area was trashed. No people anywhere. The projects gutted. Utility poles, power lines, debris, etc. all over the road. It was almost impossible to get to town. When we got down to the corner of Grand Union and Hospital, it was full of people. Two Virgin Island National Guard Girls were sitting on the corner. Natives were all trying to get into the smashed up Grand Union[25] crawling in and passing loot out. There were hundreds of them, and more coming from all directions. We asked the guard what was going on. She gave us her best Stupid White Person look. We couldn't find the Red Cross and no phones were up on the whole island. We went back to East End way. Stopped at Mario's, went past the demolished Government House, Watergate looked almost as bad as the projects, Bolongo was trashed. No more dive shop. Boats on land and sinking everywhere. Helicopters are beginning to fly over. Soon they are everywhere, but for now it is just the people who were already here. We hurry back to our safe little pile of rubble, away from the insanity of town. Mario told us they were out looting downtown during the storm. When he left his house at six AM to go check "Budget" they were already down there collecting jewelry.

Back at the house, we start sorting through the rubble. Elation when finding something that "made it". Depression when finding a piece or some clue that something was blown away. I stared and stared at the bookcase. I couldn't believe the books and videos were gone. I found my Mosbys Drug Manual in shreds on the floor under the wall. I saw a piece of my favorite shirt in a tree. I wore that shirt in San Francisco and Madison. I never did find any of my new clothes except a pair of shorts. Some still had the tags on them from my shopping trip to Atlanta the week before. I was able to save the panels with Nicks baby clothes on them. We even made a joke about the "Richie Rich Family Vault" and what's really important. We did a lot of hugging and holding those first two days. The foremost thoughts in our minds were surviving and finding a way out of here. I sent word with JoAnne that I wouldn't be back. I couldn't even consider going to work. Helicopters were flying over on day two – looking for bodies on the shores of Thatch Key. We grilled most of the remaining meat for dinner and went to bed when the sun went down.

At this point we just wanted to leave this place and began to plan accordingly. We were to soon find out that it was impossible to

---

25 Grand Union was a grocery store.

make plans and began living in the moment.

Day three. Much the same as day two, Lots of helicopters. Rodney came by. Lori's friends stopped by and then at four PM she left for Miami on a Government plane. Harry was hurt and depressed so we drank and played Monopoly by Coleman Lantern after dark. I won.

Day four. Harry woke up and said he had thought it was all a nightmare and when he woke up it would be normal life. I said, "Yeah and we would all be perfect strangers." We got the generator running and had fairly cold beer. We were really living. When we finally got the TV/VCR hooked up the next morning we were STYLIN! I put in a tape and it was country video of I want a ticket that'll take me anywhere but here. Then the 25th Anniversary of All My Children where Joe and Ruth's house had been rebuilt after the tornado and all the old people were back. I cried when I saw Greg and Jenny. And Cindy die again. Also on that tape was a little bit of "Young and Restless" in St. Thomas.

That day, with all our stuff packed in the truck ready to be shipped, I started working on Lori's stuff and organizing the house we were staying in.

The next night we invited Bruce and family over for pizza and a video. South Pacific.

NOTE: This was the end of the story and all she wrote. The following was on the next page:

BECKY'S HURRICANE SURVIVAL TIPS

Pack in to separate baggies clean underwear, socks, hiking boots, long pants and shirt. Sweats would be ideal. A disposable rain jacket. Cash. Flashlight with extra batteries. Hard candy. Add old towel (to urinate on if necessary) Plastic applicator tampons (the stress of the storm may bring on your period). Cardboard applicators swell from the moisture and are unusable. If you wear glasses, put hem in a hard container. Any medication you take daily and any nerve pills, alcohol, cigarettes, etc. you would like to have ASAP. Pack all this into a large bag and keep it with you.

Becky's account of Hurricane Marilyn continues in this letter to Bridesmaid. There is no date on this letter, found in Becky's effects, but I place it around early October 1995 shortly after we rented an apartment on St. Peter's Mountain. Bridesmaid lived in Atlanta at the time. I don't think the letter was ever mailed, as she expected to see Sharon in person by Christmas. I delivered it to Sharon recently.

Dear BMGF,[26]

Well, if this ain't quaint... paper & pen. No Bridaphone – no Brid-E-Mail. I just hope you get this before we get back there. The P.O. Is awfully slow these days.

Yes, guess you figured from the PM that I'm back in St. Thomas... Styles By Marilyn. The island is beginning to come back. It is one of the most beautiful things to watch. 1st the water cleared – Day 3. Then the 1st palms budded Day 5. The 1st flower – Day 4. Now it has greened up to almost normal except that the palms are not full. All the trees are blossoming. The hibiscus has come back, along with the bougainvillea and the fish.

My favorite dive site, a 200 ft. barge sitting upright and intact in 80 ft. of clear water, has vanished. The reefs I haven't seen yet. We are going diving next Sunday and enter an underwater pumpkin carving contest. The fish will probably be on us like white on rice, but it sounds like good country fun. Then we are going to the "white man's carnival". The clue word is "Texas Society." That is the word for "white only" here. So they are having country music at Emancipation Garden while locals do their thing on Main Street. It is celebrating the 1st cruise ship back.

Everybody is getting happier around here. We got a nice undamaged apartment next door to our friend Eric on St. Peters

---

26 Code for Bridesmaid Girlfriend. This letter is written to Sharon Rivera who lived in Atlanta, Georgia at the time.

Mountain. I can see clear to Virgin Gorda and the sunsets are too good for words. Harry has a main line connection to Frankie J. so we are stylin. Today we got full power. Lights at the slight movement of a finger. No filling the lantern or the generator. The complex went on a huge generator. This is a Texas Society place for sure. You have to be recommended to get in.

Nick is working 12 hr. days. My routine is to drive him to the Marriott at Frenchman's Reef, eat breakfast, go to K-Mart. They are having a total liquidation of goods sale 50% today. All the Texas BBQ Society items are still in full stock. No rap CDs but lots of Streisand and Tony Bennett and Pink Floyd. All the tourist stuff, white woman colors of make-up, hairspray, Jack Daniels, educational toys, self-help books, Dockers pants, anything in that chocolate brown color you like so much, and Martha Stewart Decorating books. So I shop till about 10:00 when it starts getting dark and sweaty and I head to the pool to lounge and talk to other Resort Rats and FEMA types and play with my boy. He's swimming like a pro. Then Nick brings us home, N_2 takes a nap, I visit F.J. And pick up a bit, maybe do laundry, or sumfin', and cook dinner at night.

So, I can't complain. Life's pretty good for me and I know others are suffering but that's not my burden. We lost as much as anybody. Even with all the stuff I've bought recently at K-Mart, we still won't have enough stuff to exceed the baggage limit. Life's funny sometimes ain't it? You just never know when the wind might just blow it all away. Thank God we left a lot of stuff in Florida.

Our big plan is to leave here December 2 or 3. Go to Orlando for a week of sterile, perfectly normal American squeaky clean everything matching fun.

I really worry for the homeless who don't have American Express. I can deal with sponging off the government and charity if I know I can still charge stuff. We got vouchers from the Red Cross for several hundred dollars in clothes, shoes, linens, cooler, food, and cleaning supplies. I don't feel bad taking it, except that I know I can replace a lot of stuff easier than a lot of the islanders. But then remember that these people are the ones who were out there looting and acting like a fool. "White Men Can't Loot" a new film by Marilyn Lee.

Just call me Louise. Where do you go for that delicious canned pig – only 60% FAT?

I'm going to be the first in line when K-Mart re-opens and I'm going to use my $150 voucher for a set of Martha Stewart Sheets and comforter and everything. All in blue because it's still my favorite color.

Tomorrow is a big day because Plaza Extra is getting produce. I'm going there instead f K-Mart. I am dying for a good salad.

I really had fun in Fajardo. You were right about the hotel in Dorado – a real Resort Queen delight. Tara had never been there. We also saw a couple of movies, rented some, watched stories (That ugly old Liza Colby is back and Girlfriend she is causing some trouble for Tad). It is the time to be watching and taping that soap opera for this, de fat ole cowgirl wanna be. I would love you forever, if you would tape and send weekly. It would positively be cool. Also a few Young and Restless segments would be cool. Eric has a TV and VCR. His folks sent him Seinfeld and Friends from last week.

So when we leave Orlando we want to rent a place in the mountains somewhere close to Helen would be nice. Look for us something and will make out arrangements, Dec 15 – Jan 15. We want a place with a view, secluded, 2 bedroom, 2 bath, jacuzzi, washer and dryer, fireplace, comp. Furnished with linens, etc. In that order of importance. It should have at least 5 of those 7, and be close enough to drive to do some bridesmaiding, but the further up the mountains the better. I don't care about electricity and running water – both optional at this point. So kind of keep your eyes and ears open and look for us a deal. OK?

Also if you can help me with clothes for N_2. He needs size 4 winter clothes. Ask around for hand me downs. Nick and I have clothes in J-ville.

This is really a rare opportunity for me because I get to pick where we are going to live and N can stay with FEMA on call. So you know how I love islands nd coastal places. Well I'm thinking about South East Alaska. It's sort of a compromise – not as far away as real Alaska. Not middle America. We are saving that for those formative elementary years. I'm also thinking about San Padro Texas. It's just that I'm so drawn to Alaska. I could just get a job in a Community Health Center or MD's office or do visits and work school hours and then life would just go on when Nick is on a disaster call. He likes FEMA, except that you get a lot of government pin head types.

I want to open a restaurant called "Hurricane Alley" and have all disaster pictures of hurricanes and have dishes from a region hit by a hurricane and named after it, like for example. The Hurricane Camille in Mexico – My chicken Mexican dish served on a bed of lettuce with salsa and sour cream on top. The Hurricane Hugo, Charleston style – low country shrimp and rice, cole slaw, cornbread and banana pudding.

Well you get the picture. I planned this in the beginning of the storm. I knew how bad it was going to be. You go to bed one night and the next morning you come crawlin' out of your hole to find your whole world destroyed. It was intense. These were very intense times during and just past the storm. I tried to get to work on Sunday but the looters were blocking the road and this ok white girl ain't driving through a throng of people to get to a $15.00 an hour hell hole. I repeat HELL HOLE even B.M. (Before Marilyn).

Well it's just about time for me to get up off my lazy ass and watch the sun set.

Love,
BMGF

While Becky retreated to Puerto Rico, I worked for FEMA. One day Chuck, Tara's husband, shows up with a ditty bag full of goodies: candy treats, whole pepperoni sausage, cheeses, crackers, just the kind of stuff you like to nibble on while you're working. The note on the next page was included.

Hi Honey Bunny,

I hope you enjoy all these goodies. I can't wait to see you this week. We both miss you a WHOLE LOT. Call me whenever you can.

I'm so proud of you for working so hard to get us out of this mess. I feel like we are going to recovery quickly and go on to the next great adventure. We still have our spirit & our love. Nothing can blow that away.

I love you.

Bunny

These three pictures are frames of a card Becky sent me:

This was on the cover, and when you opened it up, there was the picture and the poem on the next page.

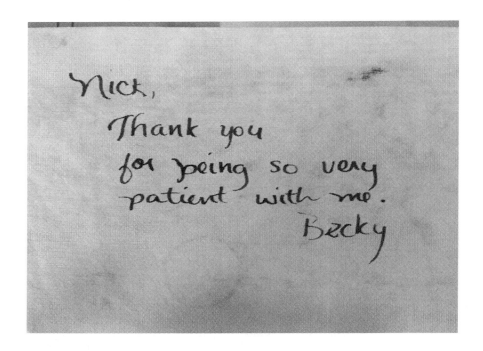

The gypsy soul in this woman
finds happiness
exploring the depths of passion
scaling the cliffs of love
found only in the heart
of an honest man.

        I love you,
         Becky

POEMS AND WRITINGS FOR BECKY

I wrote this for Becky when the Roanoke Times announced a contest for stories about acts of kindness. Becky was the kindest person I knew. It won honorable mention.

Kindness, Always Kindness

Take not kindness for grated. A gift most precious, do not confuse it with love, for without kindness, love would have no voice in which to sing its praises.

A mother stops to buy groceries: some vegetables, a carton of milk for her child, day old bread marked down to a more palatable price. It's hard to make ends meet these days. As te total displays at the register she realizes too late that there is not enough, even after mining for change at the bottom of her purse. The only thing left to do is pull some items aside and put them back, maybe that can of soup or that frozen pie thrown in the cart just because it was on sale. Before the words are uttered, before any choices are made, a stranger's hand comes forward, dropping a five dollar bill onto the stack of coupons the cashier is holding. "Keep the change," is all the stranger says before disappearing in the confusion.

"You can save someone's life with what you have learned here," says the teacher. The students know she speaks the truth, they have heard stories of kids who know what to do in an emergency, unafraid to administer CPR or put a towel over a gaping, bloody wound. It's all a matter of knowing what to do, of being trained. They thank the visiting teacher for giving then the gift of knowledge, rewarding her with a small rose bush they have bought out of their collection of spare lunch money.

Her father lies ill. Pieces of him have been removed leaving him with a colostomy and a few unchecked, cancerous growths that refuse to leave easily. Death lingers nearby, stalking like a hunter in winter, relentless, exposed, and ever closer. It would be easy to give up now, but the cool feel of the cloth on his head, the silent ministrations of his daughter, and the way she turns aside whenever a tear clouds her eye, somehow impart strength. For this woman it is no easy deathwatch, and although, as a nurse she has sat beside a hundred others in similar positions, she knows this time it is her father. It is why she moved to Roanoke in the first place, coming home like the prodigal one because the unspoken cry for help demanded an answer. Who would have known that within a year of his death she would be reliving the scene, this time with a close friend. Even in an unkind world, she continued to give kindness.

Stranger, teacher, caregiver. Five hundred words are not enough to say it all, and they cheapen the truth behind the act of kindness. I must admit that the kindest person I know is my ife Becky. She is all these things, true to the brief that random acts of kindness have meaning in today's world of violence and pain. And the greatest kindness she gives to me every day is the pleasure of her life. By example, she has made me a better person. It is at this time of the year that I am most grateful, for without her selfless devotion (and a monumental amount of work) I doubt Christmas would be complete.

Valentines Day Y2K

On a beach with stars overhead
I find myself dreaming of life with you
        May I never wake up from this dream.

Globl warming begins from the heart
Touching each other, flames burst and start
We grow tangled like vines, never apart
        Beside me there's you.

Some may claim that marriage is dead
That most of the world is better unwed
But I don't pay attention to what is said
        Because I have you.

In this big – wide Universe
I am a lucky grain of sand
To have landed beside you.

Understand this:
          Beauty is.
It is not found in a pretty face, or body,
          But through the eyes
                    Which see out if it.
It is not found in apiece of art,
          But in understanding
                    the artist.
It is not found in a mirror
          But safely hidden out of sightseeing
                    in the heart cave of love.

Beauty is not a flower
          which you can pluck whenever you wish to.
It is a moment
          frozen in time
     which
                    stands
                    out
          because life has bordered
                    it in contrast.

Beauty is not found.
          Beauty is.
          Beauty.

This one's from Jay, found in the Untimely Death Box

Becky
If you
Try To catcs
RAINbows

Sometimes
you only
end up
with Handfulls
of Air

And sometimes
you learn To fly

the world Turns
To slowly
To stand still

fly woman fly!

Odds and Ends

Yes, there are always some odds and ends. These items were in the Untimely Death box. Enjoy.

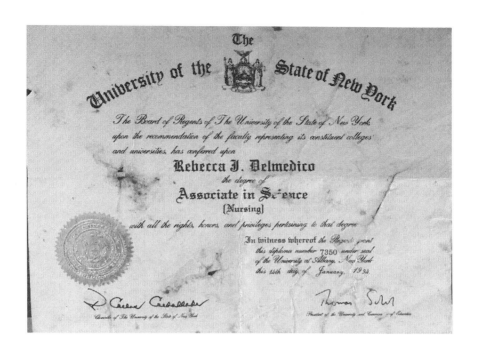

There's a story to go along with this one. We decided to cut our own tree one year and this was the choice. The tree was slightly lopsided and it was jury rigged to the ceiling to keep it up. Becky decorated it with her usual finesse and attention to detail. She always did a stunning Christmas tree. We had so many ornaments that she started decorating two trees every year: a traditional tree and a whimsical one. Anyway, the ceiling bolt came loose sending the tree crashing to the floor. She broke down crying, but Nick and I picked it all up, set the trains up again, and repaired the damage. Becky's smile returned and Christmas came as usual.

Becky Delmedico

1952 - 2017

Here's to an incredible life!

Made in the USA
Columbia, SC
28 May 2022

61045500R00126